LOVE AND MEMORIES

THE POETRY
OF
ISADORE SEEMAN

ISBN 978-0-9816804-2-2

PREFACE

The Words of a writer i

SHIRLEY: LOVE AND ANGUISH

J'Accuse 1

If I must say good-bye 2

Rendezvous 3

How can I love thee less 4

If you dare doubt 5

Testament to my love 6

How would you have me love you 7

Plea to my love 8

Sonnet on seeing my love as a babe 10

I have a message for my love 11

My love is 12

Alone 13

The trap 14

Love's new freedom 16

We live what we are 17

We have each other, too 19

Love and joy 20

1996 Valentine's Day 21

What shall I do with my memories 22

At the heights, to my love 23

Why do I love you 25

TUBERCULOSIS

- Fulfillment 26
- Quatrain 27
- The song of TB 28
- Song of the cure 29
- Pulmonary prison 30
- TB limerick 31
- It's best for the chest to rest 32
- From a tubercular bed 33
- TB caution 34
- A TB saga 35
- On the death of one long ill 36
- No monument marks the day 37

CREDO

- Credo 38
- Invitation 39
- Absolution 40
- Who am I 41
- When the game is done 42

GRANDCHILDREN

- Ode to Laura 43
- Annie and her books 45

Ode to James Michael Seeman 46

GIRL FRIENDS

The sinking of the sofa 47

On seeing Gerry in Washington 48

MISCELLANEOUS

The decadent intellectual 49

The ballad of Title VI 50

Silver anniversary 52

In virgin forest 54

Vacation 56

Where is God 57

Weep for birth and for death 59

In the land of Israel 61

Fickle muse 62

A dance of words 63

At the Pacific beach 64

Eternity 65

Life is itself 66

Life is more- a sequel 67

At 90 68

A poem 69

ODES, TRIBUTES, AND LIMERICKS

Ode to SART at Mars Hill 70

The saga of UNC elders 72

Sam's ode to Venice 75

Ode to Beethoven 78

Ode to the Elderhostel at the University of Judaism 79

Our tribute to Judy Fabrikant 81

Joe's retirement 82

Ode to the Cohen "mishpachah" 83

Ode to Leon Bernstein 85

Ode to the Bialek Club 86

A tribute to Jules at eighty 88

Ode to Shirley at 75 90

On our 50th 93

Ode to Shep 96

ON HER DEATH

Looking back 97

Never 98

Empty 99

Still me 100

Death 101

I am one 102

Mother's Day 103

Without her 104

The unseen courtyard 105

Why 107

Me 108

Not 90 109

She died 110

By Shirley's grove 111

Flowers on her grave 112

The death alphabet 113

Not good-bye 114

I am consoled 115

If she were here 116

Looking forward 117

Shirley 118

CHAPTER II: MARILYN

With you 119

Precious 120

We have each other 121

How I miss you 122

You are beautiful 123

There is the ocean 124

Valentine's Day 125

Missing you 126

We two this summer 127

Before and after 128

Longing 129

To Marilyn 130

We two 131

I am loved 132

I am not alone 133

Marilyn and the sky 134

THE WORDS OF A WRITER

These are my words,
The words of a writer
Seeking, hoping for brighter
Days, listening for songs of birds
Awakening at dawn.

These are my songs
Without tune, songs of yearning,
Thoughts burning
As my heart longs
To speak.

Set it down to remember
Times of joy and of pain.,
Hopes realized, desires in vain.
Dreams in September
Fulfilled, or shattered in May.

The moments of passion
Must not be forgot.
When the iron is hot,
Strike it, thus fashion
An everlasting memorial.

Let the muse have her way.
I open my soul,
Set down my goal,
Strive to say
What cannot be repressed.

This world, this life,
Filled with longing,
Hopes for belonging,
And fraught with strife
We seek to comprehend.

All we can know
Is what we live
What we can give
We must show
In our words and our deeds.

The words of beauty
Should be set down.
Should become renown.
It is our duty
To speak the rhyme of joy.

The times of despair
Call out for expression.
All the power in our possession
Cannot repair
The pain of sad times.

Against the background of music.
The voice of the spirit,
I listen to hear it
In words. Then be quick
To capture it forever.

The enemy is time.
It rushes away.
Day follows day,
Without reason or rhyme.
We are here, then are gone.

Fulfillment, completion is what we are seeking,
To dream, yet to make it.
To come to the chasm, and overtake it.
Hence these words we are speaking
On paper.

With all humankind, I yearn for peace
Though around us the wars
Rage on. Nations settle their scores
By arms, without surcease.
Yet my hope springs eternal.

My words are their best
When I speak of my love.
No song I can sing rises above
That ultimate test,
To open my heart.

The floodgates of passion
Open full wide
When the yearning inside
Demands that I fashion
A song of love.

I have lived for years eighty,
Now prepared for the end.
I can leave, but first send
My message so weighty,
How I loved only one.

A love words alone
Can never convey
Over and over, I try to say,
Yet ever bemoan
It falls short of expression.

A feeling so deep,
It wells up to be told
Like poets of old,
I weep
To be heard.

Try as I may,
I can never create
The gift for my mate
I strive to convey.
I love you for all time.

                                                    Isadore Seeman
                                                    July 13, 1996

SHIRLEY :

LOVE AND ANGUISH

J'ACCUSE

Stand you in judgment! Offer your defense
For these, your crimes, which now I do submit.
Most damnable and pardonless offense,
Premeditated murder; then commit
That double deadly sin, rejoice therein.
Slain is the dream of her my thoughts did bear
As she whose image would be my heart's twin.
That hand that did the deed raise now and swear
Repentance for the act. Bold robbery then
Must weigh upon your soul; your guilt confess
For stealing, dead, her very heart. Again
Atone for this, your crime, without repress.
    Your sentence: condemnation to my love.
    Denying this, fear judgment from above.

March 4-9, 1940

IF I MUST SAY GOOD-BYE

When that which thou gavest me I have no more,
That I gave thee cannot be yours, dear heart,
Knowing our love has lost its deepest core - -
Take you your leave; I mine; so let us part.
He is a man who well can say farewell;
No sad and sorry lingering, and long.
What we have been, I ne'er shall cease to tell,
What is not now I shall not drag along.
You should be cruel to let me linger on
Offering a love -- but to your heart in vain.
You should be cruel to give a love that's gone;
To leave me would be love, and bring less pain.
    Love must bind two in solemn tie.
    One lost, then both were best to say good-bye.

May 29, 1940

RENDEZVOUS

There is a shrine my soul shall e'er revere,
A sacred wooded temple. IN THAT PLACE
My heart did burn so; time can ne'er erase
The vision which my memory holds so dear.
There did I speak of love to her, so near
In heart, so near to me in close embrace.
Where better than by stream, calm current's chase
To carry off my each repressed tear.

We stood aloft there as we sat that day
And talked of earth and sky, of God and man;
Stood high above where love alone holds sway,
In the dominion of "I dare, and can
Be what I will to be." - - since I obey
The dictates of my heart, my head, and hand.

June 14, 1940

HOW CAN I LOVE THEE LESS

Doest thou stand in awe before my love?
Do I hear your protest - - of the depth,
The breadth, the very compass I proclaim
To love thee with? Give me but leave to prove
My words are but the shadows of the wealth
Of love that I would crown on thee. My very aim,
The dedication of my life and being:
To your own happiness and my own seeing
      A life with thee
      In utter ecstasy.

I cannot love thee less, nor otherwise
Than with the full deep passion of my soul.
Life on this earth is far too brief and dear,
To cast away one atom of the prize
We men are heir to. Thus the very whole
Of my dear life I pledge to share; and bear
For thee the bottomless and roofless love,
From lowest hell to highest heaven above.
      Doubt not this truth - - `
      My life shall be its proof.

                                      July 23, 1940

IF YOU DARE DOUBT

When swirling thoughts course swiftly through your mind,
And leave confusion, wonderment, and doubt,
In place of mind's peace; turn about,
My love, and lead your thoughts to look behind
The veil of questions whose dark shadows blind
You to my everlasting love. From out
Of your abyss, my love divine shall rout
Each smallest demon; then draw forth and bind
Your soul but nearer to my heart than e'er
Before it dreamed. Ensuring peace, serene
As forest's majesty when tempests tear
Their futile forces through the unyielding scene,
Shall teach your heart - - again it cannot dare
Doubt my eternal love - my heart's own queen.

July 30, 1940

TESTAMENT TO MY LOVE

Deep have I sunk,
  and felt the very floor of endless hopelessness;
Thought to have dug
  my own mired pit of black despair,
Below the ken of suns
  That man must see to see
The light; beneath e'en hope
  Of hope to e'er return;
Then deeper yet, and deeper still
  Have borne my leaden soul,
Until the dread dark door
  of very death, the final fall,
Seemed like the light,
  And sole hope
Of once more being master,
  or no more.
Then came my love with love,
And like to nothing
  that the earth or men upon it
May e'er know
  or ever dream to know,
The love which she and I
  have built with timbers of our souls
Did find me out
  e'en in my bottomless pit
And step by step, by small degrees,
  Did raise me up
To stature I once knew, and taller still
  Than e'er I hoped to be.
Here now do I stand,
  challenging the sun's own glory,
The radiance of heaven
  And man's own joy,
Noble - - bold testament to my love.

May 21, 1941

HOW WOULD YOU HAVE ME LOVE YOU

How would you have me love you? Here I stand,
My ear attuned to hear, heart to obey
Your soul's desire - -its word is my command;
My very life is yours - - if you but say
That you will have it so. Yet must I hear
That voice from deep within your heart's hidd'n core
Proclaim its will - - the thoughts that are most dear,
Most secret, most divine - - my pledge to you
Achieving, then, that love by your wish blessed,
Is my life's dedication. Yet my hand
Cannot take yours from deep within your breast.
Extended, offering in it all your love.

Let me but love you with the love I know.
The seed of yours will ripen, then, and grow.

                                                    Summer 1940
                                                    May 23, 1941

PLEA TO MY LOVE

Let me help to build you a soul.
Let us, together, descend to the base
Of the feelings that stir your heart;
There let us lay the foundation,
Deep and firm as a master mason;
Then build upon it, with science and art,
In rising planes, each set on its place,
To the lofty peak that is our goal.

Come, give me your hand, as we descend
To seek the flame which eternally lights
The paths of more than corporeal men,
The bodies that house a god.
Let us follow the course they have trod,
Disdaining more mortal glows.
Give me your hand as we climb to the heights
Where darkness conceals our end.

Let me help to show you your god;
She lies latent within the grasp of possession,
 Eager to serve you till death.
Eager to turn your potential to service,
Mold shapeless hopes into synthesis,
Awaken your dormant dreams gasping for breath,
And lead you to welcome each new-risen sun
With desire for new-birth, as a seed from its pod.

Come, give me your hand as we analyze
The motives and feelings beneath your breast,
The thinking within your mind;
Leaving no stone unturned.
Yet worthless the pursuit until we've returned
To gather the threads we have left behind,
Each element where it lies best
In a faith we shall deftly synthesize.

Let me help you to find your faith.
Without it no living is worth the name,
No value possessed of meaning.
Each must rely on a charter he's fashioned,
 The source of strength, and the base of impassioned
 Ambition and will to make real the dreaming

You've dreamed since the hour when you became
That mature and adult soul, your living wraith.

June 13, 1941

SONNET ON SEEING MY LOVE AS A BABE

That smile's contagious; or is it just to me?
Contagious, too, that mother's smiling pride.
Proud am I of what's come to be,
As she, too, must be of her smiling child.
Within that infant body, held so high,
So lightly with such delicate care and love,
And back of each small half-closed squinting eye,
Betraying smiling child's joy, parted lips of
Glee to children only known, all these
Are she as child whom now I call dear wife.
From this untutored soul, by small degrees,
Has come my love, here novice to this life.
      Thus from acorn does the tall oak grow;
      From this latency - - the love I know.

                                      November 11, 1940
                                      May 30, 1941

I HAVE A MESSAGE FOR MY LOVE

I have a message for my love.
With weighted words my tongued pen
Shall speak my heart's delight.
Flow on, you sweet and ceaseless thoughts;
Nor time nor distance dim your voice,
Telling of heavenly joy.

I have a message of my love.
I sing my song in earthly key
That should be sung above.

I tell her of treasured hours spent
Close in embrace; dear hours spent
Reliving precious dreams.

You have my message now, my love,
And with it, too, my heart and soul,
At rest beneath your breast.
In measured tune my words are set.
I know no other art to give.

MY LOVE IS -------

My love is a pyramid, tomb of thy soul,
Built for eternal enshrinement;
Here can I worship thee, priest to thy will,
Serving in humble content.
Massive the masonry, firm the foundation,
Apogee peaked in the sky.
Eternal my vigil at love's sacred station,
Entombed let me live -- here die.

My love is a stream, swiftly flowing to seaward,
Straight the channel and deep;
Damned by no ebbing, tide onward spurred
To a flood no levee can keep.
Fed from the heavens, kissed by the sun,
Passing through green and by brown,
Each droplet sacred, blessed every one;
Buoyant you swim, never drown.

My love is a pillow of featheriest down,
Cushion to thy weary soul,
Ever in readiness thy head to crown
With soft peace, enduring and whole.
Tender to soothe thee; silken, to sleep;
Drugged whisperings for thine ear;
Tranquil they spirit, then, lasting and deep,
Secure in my love, persevere.

December 19, 1940
May 21, 1941
June 13, 1944

ALONE

Sitting alone where once I sat with her,
I opened my lips to speak, but she was not there;
My eyes looked into the vacant air she had filled,
Her form beside me gone, her soft voice stilled;
My arms ached with their heavy emptiness,
My arid heart parched the tears I could not repress.
There was a lonely tree I had given her name,
Its sight to me brought feelings ever the same;
Close by were twin trees we had called our own,
Each now seemed leaning to wish to stand alone.
She was gone whom I had asked to be my wife;
Where now was the meaning I had found in life?
Alone I sat, trying to understand
The cosmos crumbling by a withdrawn hand.

June 14, 1941

THE TRAP

Life is a trap. We do not ask to come,
But screaming, we must exit from the womb
And enter this imponderable tomb,
This grand enigma, world we cannot plumb.

Nor can we choose the time when we shall go.
Bound by the laws of nature and of chance,
We're doomed to play the play, to dance the dance.
Seek no escape. The trap has willed it so.

To stay is to be caught in deep travail,
To go is to negate what brought us here
And trade this earthly hell for hells to fear.
Between the two we're trapped, to moan and wail.

Turn right and there we find the way is barred
By walls and fences insurmountable.
About face, there, incalculable,
By monsters and by dragons we'll be charred.

Climb up and up and at the top is found
Impenetrable barriers of stone.
Retreat, and down below, there all alone
Into a pool of blood we're surely drowned.

Move forward - - see the fearful sight now loom
Before your eyes - - the fires of hell on earth.
Flames leaping high, no lack, no dearth
Of red hot ashes certain to consume.

Retreat and face a greater enemy
Than all the torture physical - - the pain
Of mental anguish. Know that they are vain,
Attempts to escape this mental slavery.

Why am I here? Why born into this life?
Who is to say the purpose of this game?
No man can fathom it, give it a name,
Except to know it is Gethsemane.

Life is dilemma, two paths both bearing horns,
Between the two no passage, no wide gap
Through which we can escape this mortal trap.
"Surrender", comes the cry, "Give in", life warns.

LOVE'S NEW FREEDOM

Come, love, and we shall walk this earth, we two,
Hands joined, hearts joined, inseparable as one.
Together we'll discover and renew
The passion and the joy that once we knew.

Free of the ties that fetter and restrain,
Our bondage to the past we do renounce.
No more to sing the burdened old refrain.
A new song shall proclaim our new-won gain.

Herald new freedom, liberty declared.
Rejected all the sad and lonely ways.
We pledge new faith, our deepest love now bared.
We shall rejoice, new challenges now dared.

No fear, no caution, no enslaving past
Can stay our will to fashion love anew.
We sail ahead, love sturdy as our mast,
Joy and fulfillment promised us at last.

              May 14, 1987

WE LIVE WHAT WE ARE

Who am I?
How came I here, where I stand now?
Know this : I am me, and ever shall be.
I may become more of me as I do grow, develop, experience more of joy and of pain, observe life and live it;
But ever me I shall be -- no other.

I cannot change.
Man cannot change.
You cannot change, though change you would.
Not change yourself to someone you would be, nor change into another he or she.

How we do grow we never know.
For we are shaped in times and ways we cannot plumb.
Begin at the beginning, when we are conceived of her and him.
Conceived we are, but with no conscious state to know in what state we are conceived --
Out of love or out of accident when sexual desire is in full sway - we shall never know.

Thus genes united, hers and his, are our beginning.
Genes we never know nor fathom nor comprehend.
Nor have we learned yet from science what force genes have when forces after hold sway.

For once born of woman, we live in this world,
The world of mother and father,
And soon the world of sister and brother,
And cousins and aunts.
Into a world shaped by many --
At home, at school, at play --
Shaped by the neighborhood friends, or lack of friends,
By the grocer and the librarian, by the teachers, good and bad,
By the doctor or lack of doctor,
Shaped by the money our families have, or do not have.
Shaped and turned and fashioned and bred,
Values instilled or left untutored,
Emotions tutored or left untutored, emotions strong or emotions repressed, frustrated, crushed;
Intellects sharpened or intellects neglected, suppressed.

At the root, the love we know or the love withheld.
Parents love or parents fail and give no love.
And we are the victims or we are the fortunate,
To be loved or not to be loved,
      That is the question.

Loved, we can thrive, grow, mature, and learn in turn to love and be loved.
Left unloved, we spend our lives unloved and unloving.

Lives lived alone, or in tortured pairs,
Struggling, passions beating against passions,
Sans understanding, sans comprehension.
Petty peeves and petty differences grow and grow
And the gaps grow and the chasms widen.
We drift apart.
And the day may come when we divorce apart,
Or the days may go, and we are joined still, but unjoined still.

Oh, you who are wiser, and study Man,
Teach us, please, that we may know.
Who are we, and how came we here where we now stand?
Came to be so grossly unmatched,
So far apart, one from one.
Were we so born, and doomed from birth
To spend all years upon this earth
In loveless vein?
Or were we bred to suffer so,
Learned from all who share our lives,
Until we're dead?

Why can we not change,
Become what we would become?
What power holds us back,
Traps us in its trap,
Relentless.

Oh, you who know,
If any there are who know,
Teach us, that we, too, may know
And go our ways as we would have them be.
With joy and passion of love,
Sharing joy and sharing love.
Two who live as one, all things shared
and paired and joined
In happiness, beauty, and love.

June 29, 1988

WE HAVE EACH OTHER, TOO

We have all this, and each other, too.
A home in comfort, and a lovely view,
Necessities, and more -- more than a few.
Some are old, and some just new.
And we have each other, too.

We have fond memories, and some to rue.
Events of joy, and times quite blue.
And yet we have each other, too.

Our love was tested, and proved true,
When we were distant, we'd renew,
Become one again, where we were two.
From joy and sadness, new love grew,
And to new heights, love rose anew.
And yes, we have each other, too.

With hopes so high, together we drew,
To barriers we said adieu.
Henceforth, we pledge we shall eschew
The chasms, distances undo.
Oh, yes, we have each other, too.

You have me, and I have you.

September 23, 1994

LOVE AND JOY

I seek for love, true, lasting, and joyous.
Love that overcomes the petty trials of every day.
Every day brings small tasks, and every day demands attention to the small chores of every day.
And every day there can be petty obstacles to joy and love.
But love, true love, rides over every day's petty bumps on the road to joy.
Love should be joy.

Trials, yes. Twists and turns, unexpected and unforseen.
Life carries with it the fears and the tears of unknown paths we walk.
We know not what we will see at the next turn.
Is it to fear? Is it to awe? Is it to weep?

Who can say?
We will make the turn, and we shall know.
But along the way, there must be the open and unafraid arms, stretched out to receive what may come and to grasp it, confidently, surely, and with resolve.

No fear, no anxious wonder that all will not be well.
We know it may not be well, for tragedy is the often companion of life.
Tragic happenings happen. Tears there will be, and unhappy days and nights.
This we know.

But to know is not to fear or foretell.
For we know, too, that love is with us, and with love is joy.
Love accompanies our journey through our lives, and brings with it the joy of love.
So let us look for love and find joy.
It can be there and will be there, for us to seek and find.

I seek for love, true, lasting and joyous.
Come with me, and we shall find it or make it happen.
Together, you and I, with confident arms around each other, and a look ahead at what may come of joy or pain, ready to receive love and joy, or to deal with the pain we may endure and the tears we may shed, returning then again to the joy of love.

At the Cabin
April 1995

1996 Valentine's Day

You are my Valentine
As I am yours.

Not just this day.
For each day lures
Me to be close.

The symbol of this day - the Heart,
It beats your name, beat after beat,
Shirley, Shirley,
In steady rhythm,
Beat after beat.

So on this day, and evermore,
Together - each other's Valentines,
The love we have learned - and earned,
Evermore.

Shirley and Sam

WHAT SHALL I DO WITH MY MEMORIES?

If no one else knows the joys I once knew, are they real?
If no one shares, is it there?
I remember her,
      But she can no longer remember
      For she is only a memory.
What shall I do with my memories, alone?

We had ecstasy.
      And wept, too, beyond control.
I remember each feeling.
      I recall the time, know the day, see the place of each.
The visions are carved deep in my mind, beyond erasing.
      They rise and I know them again.
      They were real; my experience.
But can I be sure, if no one else knows?
Am I only remembering that I remember?

There is music against the sky as I lie and muse.
I am alone, with only the sky and the music - -and memories.
Shall I sing the memories? Can I paint them? If I write them
      and no one reads them, are they real?
As memories alone, they are nothing.
What can I do with my memories?

I can catalogue them, A to Z:
      Aching teeth to Zoo trips;
      Vacations with the kids;
      Passion in our nakedness, and tender whispers;
      The calamity of sudden death;
      Music together, on New Year's Eve.
But what after they're catalogued and counted?
They rush into being, and I know they happened, but whom
      shall I tell, to whom can I show them, who can feel them, who will know?
      Who would believe?
They are mine, but not real.

I have a safe deposit box where I keep my true valuables.
Can I keep my memories there?
      They will not stay locked up
          If I truly lock them up, they are no longer memories; they are nothing.
      I cannot bear it if my memories are nothing.
Yet it hurts deeply if they are only lonely memories.

AT THE HEIGHTS, TO MY LOVE

I know, at last, I now have reached the height
Of all I ever hoped and dreamed I might.

I pause, as pause I must before I die,
To take account of who I am, this I.

This one, this only I ever drew breath,
This I, at reckoning, before inevitable death.

Where have I been, what have I done on earth,
Through countless hours and days, years since my birth..

The time has come to assess the good, the bad,
To learn if I must sing for joy, or go so sad.

I take the measure of the years I've spent,
To learn if I rejoice, or must repent.

In this last judgment I must know the truth.
No hasty summing, no rash guess of youth.

The answer comes to me, quite loud, quite clear.
Where I do stand, I stand without doubt or fear.

One credo through this life was ever my guide,
An ethic I'd proclaim, not ever hide.

When you do leave this earth to which you came,
You must not go and leave it just the same.

Leave it a better place because you were here.
What is your legacy, solemn, sincere?

This world is far too wide, too vast
To change, to turn quite different from the past.

Therefore, fix firmly in your sights,
The vision you would see from new-won heights,

Bring change to only one, one whom you love,
Look down on only one from skies above.

If, when the game is done, you truly know,
Your mission complete, as from this earth you go,

She whom you loved, once troubled, once quite sad
From childhood, more tears than joy has had,

She whose life you lifelong deeply shared,
She, whose outlook on this life you dared

To change, to move from pain to joy,
Through deepest love you did employ,

To wipe away the tears, the fears, the negative,
Replaced by happy days, accepting the love you give.

New brighter joys, new loving ways,
Two happy souls living out their well-earned days

In understanding, sharing, passionate twin embrace,
Drinking in the pleasures of this pleasant place.

Look back upon both joy and anguish known,
And see fruits of the seed you've sown.

One person on this earth you gave all love.
She, from her depths, did truly rise above.

She and you, once two, through love became but one.
Then know, this earthly game you've won.

July 29, 1996

WHY DO I LOVE YOU?

I love you .....
I love you because .....
I love you because I love you.
I love you because you're you.

I love you because of your inner beauty -- and your beauty.
I love you because of your wisdom -- deep and wide.
I love you because you care -- care about all people, about those who hurt,
    care about justice for all people, about equality, about love.
I love you because you care about me.

Our love has traveled a long, winding course,
And we, and our love, have grown.
Grown together, and grown for each of us.
You have grown in love, and I have grown in love.
We have known and felt deep division and deep despair.
Out of these depths we have risen and grown,
Grown to high heights of joy and love and pure passion.
Together we have wept, sad tears, and joyous tears.

Out of these years together we have come to this day,
This day of lasting love that can never be lost.

Why do I love you?
Let me tell you again.....

                                                        August 14, 1996

TUBERCULOSIS

FULFILLMENT

(From my bed at the tuberculosis
 sanatorium.)

As a kiss is to coition
So my love, aborted now,

To the love in full fruition
I would weave about your brow.

QUATRAIN

The thoughts which I would burn with tongues of fire
Upon eternally unweatherable shrines
Must humbly spend their momentary hour
In fleeting passage o'er the waves of time.

November 26, 1939

THE SONG OF TB

Sing for T
And sing for B
Sing tubercle bacillus.

We're on the cure.
And mighty sure
We'll live
Though it may kill us.

1941

SONG OF THE CURE

If things look dark, and you desperately decide
It's time for the end, and you choose suicide,
The knife's in your hand; too late, with one stride –
    Look out you fool, it's your pneumo side.

If the doctors say you're negative
Because you really tried
To brave the zero weather
While the rest stayed inside,
And your chest begins to swell in justifiable pride –
    Look out, you fool, it's your pneumo side.

When you're finally discharged, and you step outside,
And you feel you're free, once again your own guide,
With one fell gesture you fling your arms wide –
    Lookout, you fool, it's you pneumo side.

When you meet the girl you love,
And you're close beside
The dear one you've asked to be your bride,
She sighed, and replied, and your arms begin to glide—
    Look out, you fool, it's your pneumo side.

PULMONARY PRISON

Still do I stand within these walls,
Prisoner to my lungs.
Still do I sing as oft I've sung
Of vain dire calls

To duty in the open field,
Where freer men may fight
For principles they choose as right.
I, deathly sealed

Within my open prison, bound
By microscopic chains.
Tyrannical bacillus boldly reigns,
Do sadly still look round

Upon this scene of mortal strife
With aching heart. Abed
I lie, a helpless soul; instead
I would devote my life

To work, which only we may dub
As end of life on earth,
The sole dear payment for our birth.
Still does fate play

Upon undesignated ones;
To guiltless will assign
To pay, quite innocent, the fine;
And oft visit the sons
With punishment their fathers wrought.
My jailor is the breath
Which I must draw to conquer death.
Nor can freedom be bought
By aught which I would gladly pay.

Imprisoned out of doors,
Immobile, I may view the wars,
Here patiently must stay.

January 20-27, 1941

TB LIMERICK

There was a tubercular gent
Who died of astonishment.
    The bugs that had clung
    To the hole in his lung,
Were gone. He had coughed 'till they went.

IT'S BEST FOR THE CHEST TO REST

If your doctors suggest
After making their test
That you need a rest
To heal your chest
It's vain to protest
That you feel your best;
Don't try to contest;
Take the first train west
      Then, brother, you're on the cure.

Just eat and digest
With zeal and with zest,
Get fat like the rest.
Lie back undressed
On your back or your breast.
Let the air divest
Your lungs of the pest
That's made its nest
Beneath your vest
      And breathe in the air so pure.

And then when you're blessed
With the news that your quest
Has reached its crest,
That you finally wrest
The unwelcome guest,
They no longer infest
The place they molest
Where they used to congest
It's your turn to attest
      Brother - you've done the cure.

    My tale is told,
    My song is sung,
    I'm breathing now
    On half a lung.

1940

FROM A TUBERCULAR BED

Life is what I remember it was -- and look toward being again.
Life is outside -- life is away.
Life is a cloud drifting by;
      Nothing now but a cloud drifting by,
      But a past and a place to go;
      Coming from somewhere, destined ahead;
      Nowhere now but here, drifting by.
Life is through that screen.

TB CAUTION

Some guys think that they rate MDs
Just because they got this here disease.
Well, let me tell you, kid, they're really screwy.
Don't listen to their medical hooey.
Tubercular pseudo-physicians
Kill more patients in all conditions
Than all bacilli tuberculosis
 Found in any diagnosis.
Take my advice - - don't pay no mind
To any stuff of that there kind.
The stuff I'm givin' you is straight dope.
You see, I know. I got it from the Pope.

A TB SAGA

Orderly! Orderly! Where is that ingrate!
Ring for 'im, can'tcha, you're a fine roommate!
    What the bell's broken? Yell, holler, scream! -- wait.
    Never mind now. Oh, Oh, it's too late!

ON THE DEATH OF ONE LONG ILL

If life is the pulse of a heart, and breath
Drawn in to nourish parent cells,
Breeding but new-parent life - - then death
Is for pulse, breath, cell and the parent the knell.
But who shall weep for the end of the clay,
To rhythm, when the song is done?
Life is not life if but living your day
Is adjudged your fee, and you leave a son
To breathe and breed. No, leave him instead
The mark of your soul on the roll of the men
To whom living was more than dust undead,
More divine than the earth it must be again.
      Life must be lived with a god in each heart;
      Flesh without faith is course without chart.

May 27, 1941

NO MONUMENT MARKS THE DAY

No monument marks the day.
    Unheeding time winds off her endless spool,
    Casting to men below
        The formless, shapeless stuff that is herself
        To reckon up and file away in clock and calendar.

This is the day, as men do reckon it.
    Since last I knew the world as home.
    This spot of earth that is my bed
        Hath half of heaven circled
        And charted out the course of sun and stars.

Full half a year hath turned.
    Day neighbor night's successor, then lives out her own
    Well counted hours, and is sent
        Below the earth, into eternal nothingness;
        New night succeeding, leading newer days.

And thus has this day come.
    No monument marks the day.
    Simply, I pause, and look into the chart
        Of days gone by, and days to come,
        And search for the meaning of time.

                                    January 7, 1941

CREDO

CREDO

Within the compass of time's hourly round,
Ere each his neighbor hour urges on,
My student soul, from eyes that look upon
Both men whose deepest vision hugs the ground
And those whose noble zeal can know no bound,
From ears attuned to melody and moan,
Does learn the spotless angels' wings to don,
And hasten then the depths of hell to sound.

You men who would be deemed worth your life,
Ere you have spent your mortal span on earth,
Set down your purpose -- serve as you'd be served.
Relentless, then, achievement take to wife;
Succeeding, you have paid your price of birth;
Then is joy just, and happiness deserved.

October 20-21, 1939

INVITATION

(Slowly and quietly, with calm power and force.)

The unroofed earth's my royal realm,
Sev'n continents my carpet.
Throughout this limitless domain
I reign as king!

All people are my subject slaves,
Through me they live their lives.
Their joy, their death I can decree.
My will is law!

The history of earth and man's
But my biography.
Nought in this world is not of me.
I am supreme.

Dear brother, will you share my home?
One simple pledge I beg:
Ask only that which you will give.
Won't you come in?

November 26, 1939

ABSOLUTION

Give me ever, Lord, the light
To see, and objectivity
To laugh aloud in just delight,
In frankness and sincerity,
At what in others seems to be
Quite censurable to my sight - -
When that same failing is in me.
Laughter alone can set it right.

May 15, 1941

WHO AM I?

I walk this earth a proud yet humble man.
I own my pride, for I have done good deeds.
I know humility, for though I can
Strive to fulfill the urgent wants and needs
Of those I love, not all my work succeeds.

I hold my banner and my standard high,
I do not flinch when challenges are grave.
I do not yield when failure brushes nigh.
Tyranny shall never bind me, make me slave.
Nor power corrupt, nor weakness make me knave.

My credo is engraved upon my soul,
As precious to me as my own good name:
I shall not kill. I do declare my goal:
This earth a better place than when I came.
What I expect of you, I'll do the same.

I share a love for every man on earth.
I seek to prove my love by deeds well done.
No sacrifice too great, striving to prove my worth,
I hope to leave a legacy, no dearth
Of labor for mankind, thus earn my birth.

May 14, 1987

WHEN THE GAME IS DONE

I kept no score in the game I played;
I know not whether I lost or won;
But if I can say, when the game is done,
Unceasingly I have obeyed
Those self-imposed laws I made
To play the game by,
I have not flinched, nor ever strayed
From stern perseverance of stern rule laid
Down e'er the game was yet begun,
Justice to all, and to every one.

January 7, 1941

GRANDCHILDREN

ODE TO LAURA

A child of my child and his recent bride is newborn.

She is a miracle of the miracle of life.

Nurtured in mother's womb, under father's watchful eye,

    From a woman's seed, in union with the seed of man,

    And born into the eternal chain of generation after

    generation after generation of peoplehood.

An heir of all mankind that has gone before, and destined to bear a generation beyond.

Yet she is Laura -- unique, unmatched, new, and different,

Different from all who have lived and died.

She is Laura -- special, and all her own,

    Her own special eyes searching her tiny world,

    Her own lovely face, flailing arms, legs exploring the air.

Her own charm, her own grace, her own joy of life.

Laura fills a unique place in the history of this world.

For I am the child of my father and mother, who each had a mother and father,

And I had a child who is now father to my grandchild,

And she is Laura.

My child bears my seed into the next generation, and his seed

    spawns the generation beyond, and the generations shall go

on.

Thus, I come from the past, yet I shall go on -- through Laura.

Laura is the miracle of life.

Laura is the joy of living.

Laura is at peace, the peace of innocence.

Laura is the hope of life and joy and peace.

                    April 8, 1991

January 1996

ANNIE AND HER BOOKS

Annie is an open book.
What you see is what she is.
Pure, genuine, honest joy.

Annie is an open book.
And her book is always open.
Annie loves books, and books love Annie.
Offer to read to her - a book,
Or don't offer, and she will bring the book to you.

Not one book, but books.
Books she loves.

When all else fails, there is a book for Annie.
There are favorites, and there are those that pass quickly.
But make it a book.

Bring her a book and Annie will smile.
That broad, beautiful, warm, loving smile.
It is contagious, Annie's smile.
Read to her, and the smile goes on.

She drinks in the words, and gives them back to you.
She swallows the pictures, and shows them back to you.

You do not need to read to Annie -
She will read to herself.
All of age two, and she reads her books to herself - or to you.
But to herself is best.

Annie is a joy
Annie is a smile.
Annie is entirely herself.
Annie and her books.
Annie is an open book.
Read and enjoy her.

Papa Sam

ODE TO JAMES MICHAEL SEEMAN

Our heritage will go on.
Today my son had a son, my grandson, James Michael Seeman,
The son of Jonathan Seeman and Laura Layman Seeman.
And Jonathan is my son.
The line will go on – the Seeman line.

I am the son of my father, who had a father.
I am the father of my son, who is now a father.
Today, the heritage of the long past is the heritage of the future.
My grandson will grow, a child in the Seeman line.
His father will teach him the ways of the world, and his mother will nurture him to manhood.
He will become a father to his sons, in the Seeman line.

Today is a joyous day.
There is another Seeman in the family of Seeman – James Michael.
Today is a day of rejoicing and celebration.

GIRL FRIENDS

THE SINKING OF THE SOFA
or
SAM SAT IN SUNNYSIDE

Spring saw Sam Seeman in Sunnyside.
Sam Saw GT.
Slowly they strolled to 47th Street,
Stood on the stair, and stared.
Soon they sat - - and the sofa sank.
So they stood, to serve and to sup.
To step out to see the sun and the stars,
The shows the city was selling.
They sat again as the subway sped
Them swiftly to Sunnyside.
Soon they sat - - and the sofa sank.
Softly they spoke; sat silently still.
But they stayed on the sofa, still slowly sinking.
Sat as the sofa sank.

I've a song to sing and a story to say
Of a sinking sofa in Sunnyside;
Of speaking and sighing and soft caress,
A song of sincere affection.
Of sharing and living, a song of life - -
So sweetly, sing with me this song of Sam
And the sinking sofa in Sunnyside.

March 28, 1940

ON SEEING GERRY IN WASHINGTON

Who sent the sun to shed its brilliant glory,
And warm our hearts, and bind them closer still:
Set with such art the setting for our story?
His praises do I sing, and ever will.
In memory are those visions now engraved,
Nor time nor added life can e'er erase;
Guarded by sentries solemnly enslaved.
To keep patrol in firmly measured pace
O'er love's dear shrine. Entombed within my joy.
No man, no thought, no deed shall e'er destroy.

Dear Gerry, to you is my song addressed.
Cherish it then, and set my heart at rest.

April 28-30, 1940

MISCELLANEOUS

THE DECADENT INTELLECTUAL

I think I shall live.
I think I shall give my heart away
To one who can feed my ego, and say
Her love for me is not negative,
But the will of a soul with freedom's sway.

I think I shall sublimate sex.
Avoid the frustration that wrecks the lives
Of hopeless neurotics with no other drives
Than their inverted Aedipus complex,
A libido that never survives.

I think I shall seek life's purpose.
I think I need a dose of indulgence
In seeking the aim of Divine Providence;
Philosophy then will engross
My attention from now and hence.

I think I shall analyze
The bond and the ties that hold my soul
To the path it follows to its goal,
With which I must never compromise,
Yes, I must seek my role.
Ah, yes, I think I shall live.

June 12, 1941

February 5, 1973

NOTE FOR: MR. FORBUSH
          MR. MILLER
          MR. CARDWELL

SUBJECT: Comment on Proposal for Direct Loan Procedures in the Hill-Burton Program (or the Ballad of Title VI.)

    Those Congressional peers, Hill and Burton,
    Said our hospital system was hurtin'.
        They wrote up a bill
        Granting millions, until
    The need for more beds was less certain.

    Then we turned to a system of loans,
    Adding subsidy to cushion the groans.
        We buy and sell bonds
        As the market responds.
    Now we have to keep up with Dow Jones.

    Meanwhile, back at Parklawn,
    The financiers were working 'till dawn,
        Devising a caper
        To market the paper.
    Attached is the plan that they've drawn.

    To concur or not to concur,
    That is the question, dear sir.
        Do we add our consent
        To the memo we're sent?
    It's an issue we cannot defer.

    While the question's before AS/C,
    Across town is heard a decree.
        There's no doubt of the source
        It is coming, of course,
    From the oracle called OMB.

    They've made perfectly clear their desire,
    Section 626 must expire.
        It all ends, you recall,
        Loans, grants, and all,
    When the mortgages written retire.

The securities now in our hand
Must be offered for bid throughout the land.
    Though we tried Fannie Mae
    It won't do, so they say,
We must peddle them as our own brand.

So let's set up the system proposed,
Though just after it's opened, it's closed.
    If we fail to do it
    By GAO we'lll rue it.
There's no point in being opposed.

This analysis may lack precision
Except for one major decision.
    This rings down the curtain
    On dear old Hill-Burton.
It will soon be only a vision.

                                          Isadore Seeman

SILVER ANNIVERSARY

Now what am I, and what are you, together what are we?
They tell me that we're here to see a silver anniversary.
Say, listen, since we're gathered here in one big happy family --
Let's let down our hair, and be lighthearted and carefree.

I am I, and you are you, and he is he, she, she.
In Hebrew, so they tell me, me is who, and who is she.
This verse is just as silly as it possibly could be,
But then who said it's sillier than you, or you or me

Shirley was a girlie with a curlie in her hair.
She had to get up early just to brush and comb and care.
But finally she got it up, in disgust and despair.
Don't look now, but there's a short strand hanging there.

Mother always had to get up early to be there
When the iceman left the ice, to be sure she got full share.
Now I'm not insinuating, you know I wouldn't dare,
But it does seem strange -- that now we have a Frigidaire.

"Now eat some bread -- it's healthy", Daddy tells us every day.
And then Mother gives him slices which he promptly puts away.
No, not in his stomach, right back on the tray.
"You should eat it, Daddy, it's got Vitamin A."

"Mother, where is Evelyn?" "She slept out last night."
"Why, good morning, dear, did you sleep alright?
You're looking very tired, though perhaps a little bright."
"Mother, take her off. She wants to start a fight."

Irvin's raising bugs. No, he's learning how to type.
I thought you said he was smoking a pipe.
Well, you're all wrong now, there's a brand new stripe --
Won't you play us a tune -- it's his new hornpipe.

(Ida)
Why, come right in, I'm glad to see you, my dear.
Look out, be sure you don't bump the chandelier.
Won't you have a chair? Now look at that smear.
Oh, well, thank heaven, the roof's still here.

(Ben)

I didn't know that the brakes still jar,
Now look how the clutch moves back too far.
The gear's not there, but the tires still are.
Who just drove up? Surprise, It's Uncle Ben's new car..

IN VIGIN FOREST

Today I walked in virgin forest
Unspoiled by the hand of man.
Self-felled trees feed the seed of new birth,
Nature's wonder beyond the ken of transient man.

Along cathedral trail I trod,
Cathedral wrought by Nature's craft,
Its spires the green of branches tall,
Its pews the underbrush grown sturdy,
Hidden from the sun, yet taught
To survive beneath majestic spires.

Along the stream I slowly strode
And stopped and listened to its voice,
Unceasing, eternal, unfathomable sound,
The song of nature and of wonder.

The giant hemlock stood so proud,
Master of its kingdom of trees, of shrubs and creek,
Host to the birds whose song prevailed
Against the distant noise of motors -- harsh intrusion of man.
I shut these out for my brief moment in the virgin forest.

Leaves of yesteryear remain,
Decaying, natures's wondrous cycle,
Each new generation nourished,
Each completed life deserted.
Gone, but passing on its heritage,
Nature's law unbreakable by nature -- or by man.

A small virgin forest stands
Where all was virgin 'till raped by men,
Their roads and shops and paperwork destroying nature's gift.

I walked in virgin forest briefly
And looked up at the sun and sky protecting this inheritance.
Precious gift of nature,
Preserved by law from ax and saw.

In awe I paused from earthly tasks,
In wonder breathed the air so rare.

In admiration I surveyed
The virgin forest here preserved.

All men should put aside their cares
One hour. Leave behind the chores and wars.
Come, walk this day
While time allows and nature still holds sway
Over virgin forest - Cathedral Park.
                May 12, 1987

VACATION

The world is on vacation.
    Lie lazily dreaming,
        Forget life's mad scheming
For wealth, for glory, and fame.

The seasons are on vacation.
    The wind gently plays
        Through long sun-filled day
Without storm, without struggle or strife.

Our scholars are on vacation.
    Philosophical quest,
        Moral thought and the rest
Are replaced by deep swimming and bathing.

Our women are on vacation.
    Their sexual purity
        Loses its surety.
Temptation's too strong in the sun.

Education is on vacation.
    What you've learned in school
        Will dub you a fool
If you practice the precepts you're taught.

Moral justice is on vacation.
    It's more pleasant to ride
        On the waves of the tide
Than determine what's wrong and what's right.

Vacations are now on vacation.
    Once again we're confined
        To the daily grind.
Forget it, you've had all your fun.

The world is on vacation
    It's time to relax
        And forget the facts.
What the hell, it's the same when you're done.

WHERE IS GOD?

Where is God?

God is in the miracle of creation.
We do not understand creation.
We do not understand God.

God is in all the wonders we see and hear and feel and do, every day.
In the beauty, all the beauty, the beauty of the flowers, red and yellow and blue and lavender.
In the grass that grows and the winter snows.
These are God's works,
For God is what God does.

God is in man and all the wonders that man discovers and invents and achieves,
In the machines we make and run, and the repairs we make,
In the rockets we send into outer space that are God's spaces, that were created by God and await man's adventures that are God's.

God is in the human spirit that is beyond the human spirit.

God is in our tears when great joy overwhelms us.

And God is in out tears when great tragedy befalls us and we sense that great power outside us that shapes our tragedies. For God can make no promises, and thus God cannot promise that there will be no harm and no suffering and no inhumanity of man to man, no promise that there will be no holocausts past and future, for these are man's works and not the works of a God. God does not promise joy alone.

Where is God?
God is everywhere. In the lightning and in the thunder that follows and in the rain that follows.
God is in the unduplicated snowflake, each snowflake, and in the rushing river and in the peace of the still lake.
The sounds we hear are the sounds of God -- the birds singing, all the variety of birds and songs,
In the bees and the pollen they carry to make new flowers, the act of creation,
In the wheat that nourishes, the cotton that covers.

God is beauty.
God is power,
The power man amasses and puts to work, the electric current, the atom, the wheels turning.
God is motion and stillness.
God is silence, too, restful silence, inner silence and outer silence.

God is in men's souls. The spirit that drives and inspires, creates art and poetry and music.

God is there when we face adversity and find our way.
God is in the new morning and the long day that follows, bright, sunny and awaiting man to do all that man can do.
And God is in the night, quiet, dark, peaceful.
In the sleep that renews, God's blessing.
The quiet night is being alone to know God.

Above all God is love and God is peace.

God is the love of one man for one woman, the love that nourishes and sustains and brings joy and happiness and wondrous union, and God is the union that brings forth the new child, to become a woman and a man to love one another.

And God is the love of one man or woman for all other men and women who are over all the earth, and who manifest God.

Above all, God is peace.
God is the peace that stills men's souls and stills men's troubled spirits and quiets the turmoil of each day.
God is the force that makes peace possible,
The justice that make peace possible,
The justice that treats all men as equals, treats in fairness and open opportunity, the same opportunity for all.
God is not merely the absence of war. War is anti-God.
God is peace.

God is behind your question when you ask, "Where is God?"
For God is the quest of man to know all that is beyond man himself, to wonder at and understand the universe.

Ask not who God is.
God is not who, God is where.
God is everywhere -- everywhere that there is wonderment, power, beauty, creation, art, love, and peace - there is God.

June 8, 1988

WEEP FOR BIRTH AND FOR DEATH

The rabbi named his infant daughter.

He invoked the ancient covenant that declared her a Jewess, another of the long line of Hebrews, descended from the union of Abraham and Sarah, the union of Isaac and Rebecca, the union of Jacob and Rachel.

The rabbi pronounced the blessing on the child his wife bore them, the blessing invoked countless and countless times over 2,000 years of Jewish joy and oppression.

His benediction closed the birth bond of her Jewishness.

And the celebration brought tears to my eyes -- tears of joy, tears of appreciation, tears of pleasure, and tears of wonder.

I wept as a new chapter in the course of humankind was alive before me.

I weep when I see a vision in my mind's eye of generation following new-born generation, spanning thousands of years past, and the thousands of years to come when new birth will renew the cycle of the life of the people -- the Jewish people and all people.

Renewal is joy, and in deep joy, I cry. I cannot restrain the tears -- nor should I try.

Men, they say, should not cry, for they are men. I cry without shame, a man born of woman, one in the unnumbered multitude of human beings linking all people to God's peoplehood. I cry without shame in the joy of my ancient Jewish brotherhood, and the hope that one day my son will bear a Jewish child to perpetuate my line of Jewish brotherhood.

Yet my tears are not reserved for joy alone.

Tears well up when the course of mankind brings death, inevitable death, as the cycle of life runs its certain course of death and birth.

I wept as I pronounced a prayer over my brother's grave, a brother I loved and lost, a brother I treasured and cared for as he lay dying, waiting for the death we both knew would come soon. I cried as I nursed him, and I cried when there was an end to nursing. I cry still each time I see his face in my mind's eye, and feel his love and my love. I am my brother's keeper.

But tears must be wiped away as time and life go on. Life is to live, in joy and sorrow, but to live.

Stand back in your holy place of prayer and view the eternal river of life. The newborn infant is named, named after a loved one who died, and the cycle of life and death flow on.

Do not hesitate to cry for the joy of birth, and cry for the pain of death.

Weep freely at the wonder of God's blessing of life for his people.

August 6, 1989

IN THE LAND OF ISRAEL

I stand here on this land,
The land where my ancient ancestors walked.
On the land where Abraham walked with Sarah, where Isaac walked with Rebecca.
On this hallowed land,
This Canaan, this Palestine, this Israel,
This Israel of the Jews of yesterday and the Jews of today.
I am a Jew, of the people of Israel, in Israel today,
On the soil of Israel,
Israel that is thousands of years old.

I awake at dawn, and listen for the first song of the first bird at sunrise, at the first light of this new
    day in Israel.
I hear the song of the first bird this day,
A song heard by the Jews of Israel thousands of years ago.
The song of the first bird is interrupted today by the sound
    of a helicopter, followed by a second helicopter's sound.
I awake in Israel of today, and stand on the land of Israel, close to its border with its neighbor,
And word comes that those who are bent on Israel's destruction seek to cross that border,
And once again helicopters are dispatched to intercept the enemies of Israel.

Why are there again enemies of Israel?
On this land the Maccabees fought to defend the Jews of Biblical Israel.
And Joshua fought the battle of Jerico.
And the Jews of Masada died in defense of Judaism.
On this land in 1948 Jews declared the rebirth of ancient Israel, and defended the land against those
    who said, "No, No Israel."
On this Israel armored tanks rolled forth against the armies of Egypt and Syria and Jordan in 1967,
    and planes of war flew across the desert to defend Israel on Yom Kippur in 1973.
This land of Israel, this ancient land of the Jews, is alert today, poised in massive defense against
    unfriendly neighbors, as in ancient times.

The people of Israel around the world look to the homeland of the Jews, Israel today, the ancient
    Israel of Judaism's birth.
Why is Israel not a safe haven for its people?
Why must the people of Israel fight and die for a home, again, again, and again?

All greet each other in Israel with "Shalom", but there is no peace in Israel.

FICKLE MUSE

How fickle is my Muse.
       Tonight she will not come. It seems my diet
       Displeases her. In vain I plead, "I'll try it,
       By thy leave." In vain! She'll not be moved.
       Nay, never! Ages of sages all have proved - -
       No Muse's wand, inspiring word, no vowel
       May rival the matchless song of an umoved bowel.

Ah, fickle Muse...

A DANCE OF WORDS

What is Martha Graham?
What is Martha Graham?

This is a poem.
These are words.
I am a poet.
I am writing these words.
You are reading these words.
(Look for the nearest exit now.)
You are reading these words?

What is Martha Graham?
What is Martha Graham?
Name me the name that is Martha Graham.
Bravo!
1940 - Martha Graham on Broadway.
1740 - Captain Miles Standish, on her mother's side.
These were the Grahams in 1740.
Part II: Indian Episode.
Pocahontas Graham Standish.

Part III: The same.
Part IV: Still the same.
Finale:
    Occupation
    Graham's relation.
    Dance recital.
    Sh-h-h-h
    MG
Loud amen!

AT THE PACIFIC BEACH

In the deep dark night I hear the never-ending waves wash ashore,
Over and over and over they break, over and over,
Sending their unique sound across the beach to my bed.
I hear the Pacific.

All night the song of the waves repeats its chorus;
A splash; then brief silence waiting for the next wave to break and splash ashore.
Intermittent sound and silence, the ocean's chorus., the Pacific song, all night long.

Sometimes high and rough and full of foamy white breakers, the tide roars in, crashing, sending an arc, a tongue far up the sandy beach.
Sometimes low and soft, slow and calm, the tide gently washes the shore.

The Pacific never rests.
All night its rhythm rends the air.
I fall asleep to the sound of the Pacific waves.
I awake and the Pacific has not slept, its new waves repeat the Pacific refrain.
I sleep again, and on awakening I hear the same Pacific song.

The sun is up, bright and warming.
The Pacific ignores the change to light, its waves still washing the same shore, now seen and heard.
The song is unchanged.
The Pacific rolls on.

I see the outer breakers now;
They roll over and pound the ocean floor, pushing new breakers to the shore.
Each wave washes up on the sand, and rolls back into the sea, ready for the next assault.
There will be new assaults.
The Pacific does not rest - ever. Never.

There is no end to the Pacific waves, each hour, each day, each night, for weeks and months and years -- for decades and centuries.
The Pacific.
The Pacific rolls on.

I walk along the shore of the Pacific, watching the waves, listening in awe of the power that creates the Pacific waves.

February 11, 1995

ETERNITY

Where is eternity?
Where shall I spend all the rest of the days and nights of eternity?

I cannot conceive of eternity. For I am not I in eternity. Eternity is beyond me, beyond my world.

I came into this only world that I know and shall know.
I shall leave it, and go.
Where, I do not know.
But I shall go - forever.
And forever is eternity.

Eternity is everything, and it is nothingness.
It is time without beginning, and surely time without end, else it is not eternity.

What is there that can exist for eternity?
Not the earth, for it came into being, and will disappear, so science says.
Not the sun which nourishes the earth, for it was born and it will die.
Everything that is born dies - except eternity, which lives forever.
But what is forever?

When did time begin? How did time begin. Where was nothingness before time?
When was there a time without time?

When will time end? What comes after the end of time?

I will not live to see eternity.
I shall die on this earth, and what remains shall be of this earth for eternity.
But then it is not I.
How will I endure the length of eternity, the emptiness of eternity, the nothingness, the timelessness, the hollow, barren, timeless time of eternity?
I walk this earth, and live it, I, the only I there is, and the I that shall not be into eternity.
Eternity shall go on, without me.

I yearn for eternal existence, knowing eternity escapes me.
I can see eternity, but it is beyond me, unreachable, unattainable.
My days shall end, and then I shall be no more.
All that I was, that I did, that I hoped and dreamed shall be no more.
And my eternity shall begin, without me.

In vain I yearn for eternity.

July 1, 1996

LIFE IS ITSELF

Life is itself.
All of nature gives perpetual testimony.
Every living being - yes, every living thing tells us that life is itself.

The Emperor Penguin, in the unimaginable cold of the Antarctic, travels miles and miles - back and forth – to give birth to new life.
The Penguin does not ask why. He and she live and breed chicks that live and breed chicks. They do not wonder why.

The robin returns year after year to her nesting place to lay her eggs and hatch new robins.
The robin does not ask why. They fly miles to breed chicks that live and fly and breed chicks. They do not wonder why.

The salmon swims to the sea, then struggles upstream to return to breed salmon that swim and return and breed salmon.
The salmon does not ask why, does not wonder why.

A flower blooms and sends out seeds and new flowers grow where the old flower dies.
The flower does not wonder why.

I am the son of my mother and father, who had a mother and father, and I am the father of my son, who has a son who will be a father.

We birth new children who grow and birth new children.
Why do we ask why?

Life is full of joy and deep sadness, of passion and grief.
Life is full of life, and life gives way to death after the birth of new life.

Life is itself.

September 25, 2005

LIFE IS MORE – A SEQUEL

Life is itself –save for us, we humans.

All that lives gives birth to new life, and dies, leaving new birth to give birth and die.
All that lives breeds new life, and most does not ask why, does not wonder why.
Save for us.

We who are conscious that we live and die, we ask why.
The human mind asks why.
Why am I here; why was I born?
Since I will die, why?
Is there something I must do to earn my birth, before I die?

Each asks the question, in his way (or not at all).
Each answers, in his way (or not at all).

Is there, then, an answer? Why?
Desperately, I try.
Is there an answer? For me? For all?

No answer comes from nature, no answer from science.
I search for an answer, why?
And out of deep and urgent thought, searching the soul, reading the history of humankind, comes an answer.
What do we owe ourselves and our heirs?
Is there a mission, a purpose in it all?

We were born and we will die. What do we leave behind?
We leave those whom we gave birth to, gave life to. Life is itself.
But what more do we leave behind besides life?
We must leave behind the work we did to leave it better than we found it.
That, for me, is why.

What is why for you?
What is why.

October 23, 2005

AT 90

David and Jonathan and Philip,
Kathy and Laura and Diane,
Laura and Anna and Jamie,
These are my fabulous treasures.
With them I survive life's travails,
With them I regale in life's pleasures.

Three sons I am proud to have,
Precious daughters-in-law come with them.
Grandchildren, a marvelous plus.
Each of us receives his measures;
Each is allotted his trials,
Each is permitted his leisures.

My long life it is time to assess,
What of genuine value I possess.
For my errors I make amends,
What I hold dearest – family and friends.

August 2006

A POEM

I string together thoughts and words,

And behold, A POEM.

                                             October 31, 2011

ODES, TRIBUTES, AND LIMERICKS

ODE TO SART AT MARS HILL

There once was a company called SART,
Renowned for its theatre art.
      Jim Thomas, its producer,
        Was quite a seducer,
Captivating the elderhostel from the start.

We each took a turn with his chair.
We saw what was really not there.
      The chair went for a drive,
        And was used for a dive,
Then turned into a house of prayer.

T. asked us - what is a play?
Then promptly went on to say
      You must want something badly,
        Pursuing it madly,
No matter what gets in the way.

Horace's dictum: instruct or delight,
As the actors perform every night.
      Rehearsing each part
        With their craft and their art
From the script wrought by the playwright.

Michael, David, Kenny and Ben
Each shared his professional ken.
      Build the character with care,
        Pretend that you're there
We learned from the skillful men.

Our playwright, C. Robert Jones,
Dissected a play, flesh and bones,
      Peter Cottontail died
        Of multiple sclerosis, he sighed.
His knowledge he shared, all he owns.

The design concept by Lynne
Is where the visual effect will begin.
      Then she gives it to Scott,
        Who like it or not,
Will build it, though he'll cuss or he'll grin.

Then into the picture comes Sara,
Her costumes ever fit the era.
      Trailed by Paula and Bob,
        Who will cut, sew - then sob,
For perfection's the goal, with no error.

To the Nancys, Gregory and Fosson,
We take of our hats and we toss em'.
      Every wish they heard,
        Whether real or absurd.
Our comforts they met without bossin

We thank Ray Rapp for his tour,
Behind the scenes he did so much more.
      Our food and our pleasure
        He arranged in full measure,
Good spirit behind every chore.

As we say our farewell to Mars Hill,
Ever grateful to T, our minds fill
      With the moment of magic,
        Comedic or tragic.
We will relish the more each playbill.

                                          June 25, 1987

THE SAGA OF UNC ELDERS

Those 42 elders, that's we,
Descended on UNC.
    We'd have drifted about freely
        In the City of Greeley.
We were saved by indomitable Nancy.

To her we owe a great debt.
We'd be foundering aimlessly yet,
    But she took us in hand
        As she organized and planned
For a week we will never forget.

To her partner, Elke, as well
We give thanks for a week that was swell.
    We admire, we revere,
        Her constant good cheer.
Her laughter rings out like a bell.

No problem for her was too great.
Each announcement was timely, never late.
    One problem alone - -
        Not hers, but our own.
We ate and we ate and we ate.

We awoke quite early, eyes bleary,
From our lecture from Dr. Ford Cleere,
    He described social class,
        He lamented, alas - -
Does democracy function? Not really.

Yes, we have two parties in name,
But in fact they are one and the same,
    Since both, as we know,
        Maintain the status quo.
We are all merely playing the game.

Dr. Koplitz followed behind
And explained the human mind.
    We recorded each theory,
        We never grew weary
Of discussing humankind.

We examined our values, and testing,
Discussed behavior, without resting.
    In turn we'd reveal
      How we think and we feel.
All the while his concepts digesting

Then onto geographer John Dietz,
Than whom none we know ever beats.
    Telling Centennial's story,
      He's covered with glory.
With his knowledge no one competes.

His perceptions, his trips, and his slides
All merit the status he prides.
    He knows the mountains,
      Exudes facts like fountains,
His love for the earth he never hides.

The UNC chef does so well,
The food, it does truly excel.
    For a meal we're never late,
      So we ate and we ate.
Don't stand on the scale, it will tell.

All three professors, barring none,
Dropped gems of wisdom, one by one.
    Our task, then, no doubt
      Is to sort it all out.
It's a challenge, but still it's great fun.

Visiting Centennial Village was our luck.
Elke said she would pass the buck.
    That turned out not to be funny
      As she collected our money.
In fact, with every chore she got stuck.

Three heads are better than one,
The trickle-down theory - -has it won?
    The lesser evil got our vote,
      We're all in the same boat.
See what Michener's Centennial has done!

Of Carl Rogers's views we're quite sure.
We know Koplitz's taste in decor.
    We admired Pawnee Butte,

None of us ever mute.
Third parties we must not ignore.

As we leave the great State of Colorado,
With one voice we shout bravo, bravo.
    Hail to you, UNC,
      Elderhostlers are we.
We have learned much more than we know.

                                          August 1990

SAM'S ODE TO VENICE

The medieval Republic of Venice,
Provoked by the barbarian menace,
    Gave birth to great arts
    Where our Elderhostel starts,
Which, of course, leaves us no time for tennis.

Instead, as we board the vaporetto,
Having heard the story of Gepeto,
    With Rosanna as guide,
    Who points with great pride --
"Oh, look, there's another Tintoretto!"

But Steve has already explained,
As he lovingly and passionately proclaimed,
    The Venetians were sensual,
    Discarding the conventional,
As each of the artists he named.

There's Bellini, both father and son,
Carpaccio painted more than one.
    Of Veronese we saw four,
    And Titian -- for sure.
Our exploration has hardly begun.

It took Steve all of one week
To describe Venetian features unique.
    The colors so rich,
    The surfaces on which
Perspective was what they would seek.

There's a special Venetian light
That makes the colors so bright.
    There's Georgione's "The Tempest,"
    Sorry, Steve, I forgot the rest.
I hope you'll say that's alright.

Oh, yes, we saw churches galore.
There were Gothic and Baroque by the score.
    There were Byzantine, too,
    In fact quite a few,
With paintings for parishioners to adore.

It didn't take very much urgin'
To show us another Virgin.
    Mary holding baby Jesu
    With angels in full view,
Giotto's reverence and talent convergin'.

Michael Knapton uncovered the mystery,
As he taught us Venetian history.
    At its height so divine,
    Then its sorry decline.
'Till today it is chiefly touristuri.

With Toni we walked around,
As we travelled the hallowed ground,
    Where, in awe, we heard
    The immortal word
Of Hemingway, Ruskin, and Pound.

Here Commedia del Arte was born,
As Stefania described one morn.
    No need for a script,
    Harlequin pranced and quipped.
As a lover he earned only scorn.

The words were set down by Goldoni,
Instead of mere clowns who were phony.
    He wrote plays that were real,
    With a musical feel.
He gave up the absurd Pantalone.

Our music instructor, Susan Moses,
Described how Monteverdi composes.
    Of innovations she spoke,
    From Renaissance to Baroque,
The first opera, Orfeo, she exposes.

Vivaldi wrote for solo violin.
The Pope almost thought 'twas a sin.
    Antonio Corelli
    Wrote concerto so belli.
Baroque music thus did begin.

We heard Susan perform on the cello,
A sound so lovely and mellow.
  We learned fugue and motet,
   Themes we'll never forget.
Vivaldi -- not such a priestly fellow.

Our stay in the Venetian lagoon
Unfortunately ends too soon.
  Filled with music and art
   And architecture from the start,
With great friends we could stay until June.

So, Steve -- we wish we could stay.
Toni, Michael, Stefania -- good day.
  To Susan and Rosanna
   Our resounding hosanna,
As homeward we wend our way.

    April 21, 1994

ODE TO BEETHOVEN

To our Elderhostel with Ludwig
We came with expectations so big.
    Now there's just one regret,
    And we're hoping yet
He'll come back and do his own gig.

We studied the symphonies, all nine,
From the Pastoral to the sublime.
    Admire their sweep and their range.
    When it seems clear, it will change.
He broke new paths for his time.

Then we heard the piano concertos
Led by Doug who showed us what he knows.
    With his scores and his charts
    You could follow the parts,
But only if you stay on your toes.

Sonatas for piano were course three.
Listen for A, then for B, and then C.
    Theme I, bridge, Theme II
    And then codas, quite a few.
Beethoven's joke on you and on me.

One thing we heard quite a lotta
Was the inevitable form - - the sonata.
    Of the structure there's no doubt.
    It is clearly laid out.
You just follow it, because you gotta.

Exposition, Development, and Recap.
That much I learned, I"m no sap.
    We heard it again and again.
    No one said - - say when.
You can't miss it unless you nap.

To Peabody we owe a great debt.
Of Elderhostels, it's a best bet.
    Instructors first rate,
    And talent that's great.
A music week we'll not forget.

December 15, 1944

ODE TO THE ELDERHOSTEL
AT THE UNIVERSITY OF JUDAISM

There once was a school in L.A.
Affectionately know as U.J.
    Its courses of study
     Are not fuddy-duddy,
They're seriously Jewish, I'd say.

Its students probe the Judaic,
Immersing themselves in Hebraic.
    Those game to try
     And not just get by,
They also attempt Aramaic.

There's a mezzuzah on every doorpost.
The food - - it is kosher, to the utmost.
    Most professors are rabbis,
     You can tell - - they wear ties.
Oh, boy, are they proud! Do they boast!

All week many questions were heard.
Some serious, some quite absurd.
    But you won't pass the test
     Till you've mastered the best - -
"Who thinks nudnik's an English word?"

When someone asked, "Who is a Jew?"
We know that it means me and you.
    But what about others,
     Sons of fathers or mothers?
Firm opinions are many, not few.

One course was on the prophetic,
Both sacred and aesthetic.
    We met Amos, Hosea,
     Jeremiah, Isaiah,
All preaching the Jewish ethic.

When a Jew has breathed his last breath,
And is taken from us by death,
    Though we feel bereft,
     Is there anything left?
What's it like in the lower depth?

Many Jews profess they're Reform,
For others Conservatives the norm.
      But to Orthodox, both are goyim,
         Oy, Veh, tyre boyim,
Renounce them! Let's kick up a storm.

Schecter and Schecter is not what you think.
Yes, it's true that there is a link,
      But it's not a law firm.
      They're both teaching this term.
They lead us to water and we drink.

Then there's Finley, and Elkins and Goor,
Not one of the profs is a bore.
      They teach unity and diversity
        And Judaism's adversity,
As the class yells, "More, we want more."

We didn't choose U.J. for math,
Nor even to seek out God's path.
      Nor was it the season.
      You know the real reason.
Who wouldn't prefer a private bath.

Elderhostlers of '91,
We not only had great fun.
      The really good news
      Is we'll be better Jews,
Because of the knowledge we've won.

As our week of great learning ends,
And we say good-bye to new friends,
      To Gail Minkow our thanks
      We've enriched our knowledge banks.
With new insights we'll watch Jewish trends.

OUR TRIBUTE TO JUDY FABRIKANT

There was a young lady named Judy,
A model of feminine beauty.
      But she's not only cute,
      She can really compute
Well beyond the call of duty.

We all attended her class
Hoping each of us would pass.
      Now we manage our data
      From Alpha to Zeta
Because we can call up SAS.

She taught us our JCL,
And our input and routing as well.
      Nothing would phase her,
      Not even the laser
Or our questions, as dumb as Hell.

We learned about PROC PRINT and TABLES,
And run them as well as we're able.
      She showed us each error,
      Relieving our terror,
And regaled us with computer fables.

We learned to insert and delete.
Running PROC FREQ was quite a feat.
      The semicolon's a must,
      SAS will never adjust,
Without it no line is complete.

They said the computer was dumb,
But I soon learned I was the one.
      Judy taught us the rules;
      They're not friendly to fools.
We persisted; we did not succumb.

Class is over. We reap what we sow.
We're amazed at what we know.
      We will generate tables
      With titles and labels.
And Judy will bask in the glow.

JOE'S RETIREMENT

There was a young man named Joe,
Whose professional repute we all know.
    It's a thing to admire,
    But he says he'll retire.
Now we say, "Joe, we hate to see you go."

There's a guy with a helmet and shorts,
Dressed up for his favorite sports.
    As he turns off the pike,
    He dismounts his bike.
With statistics he gaily cavorts.

There's a gadget they call the Atari,
Unless you can master it you're sorry.
    So we set up a club,
    With Joe at the hub;
Our computer repute is now starry.

The Mortality Followback group
Realized they would be in the soup.
    So they turned to Barbano
    A pro - - that we all know.
Now the survey is bound to be a scoop.

ODE TO THE COHEN "MISHPACHAH"

There once was a family called Cohen,
Though as Shankman they should truly be known.
    To acquire the Cohen fame
    Sol took his half-brother's name,
And the family kept growin' and growin'.

Sol and Catherine in Russia were wed,
But preferred America instead.
    They heard it was heaven
    So with children - - all seven,
They sailed the Atlantic without dread.

They arrived in 1893.
That's almost a century.
    100 years, all but one.
    Generations have come
To make way for you and for me.

In Nashville they chose to settle.
Here Solomon would test his mettle.
    In Russia he sold flax;
    Here that business was lax.
For a living, he decided to peddle.

With seven children they had to cope.
With a new language they had to grope.
    New customs to learn
    And a living to earn,
But they faced it with faith and with hope.

There was Annie, Sarah, Ralph, and Jake,
Frieda, Benjamin, Eva - - that seven, I make.
    With a family so large, parents had to take charge.
Life was difficult, make no mistake.

Now we gather to celebrate
A reunion of offspring and mate.
    Some people we knew.
    But so many are new;
Some grandchildren - - great, great, great.

It's time to meet uncles and cousins,

We are here by the tens and the dozens.
    "Hello, how are you?"
    "You're related to who?"
"I thought that was you, but it wasn't."

In all we number 188,
Thanks to Solomon and Catherine, the great.
    But you know there'll be more,
      Of this you can be sure,
As long as each Cohen finds a mate.

To Eleanor Brody we owe a great debt.
She conceived, and then cast a wide net.
    She brought the Cohens together,
      We're birds of a feather.
But you ain't seen nothin' yet.

Now we know from whom each was born and bred.
No longer strangers; close friends instead.
    We are four generations
      Of various relations.
Together, we look to the days ahead.

                              July 4, 1992

ODE TO LEON BERNSTEIN

There once was a Bernstein called Leon,
Whose like comes but once in an eon.
      He's of hospital fame.
      We can all see his name
In lights that are blazing in neon.

He ran a hospital in L.A.,
And in the midwest, too, they say.
      Then to HCFA he moved
      And once again proved
With his skill - he saved the day.

Then he theoretically retired,
But by Maryland U. he was hired,
      Where he lectured and taught
      And provoked students' thought
'Till of that, too he tired.

So now he takes courses, and cooks,
And travels, and reads many books.
      With Dorothy, spends his days
      At concerts and plays,
You can tell they're happy - by their looks.

Here's to you, Leon, at 75,
And to other birthdays you'll survive.
      We all wish you well,
      And from children to kvell.
Keep your sparkling spirit alive.

          July 17, 1993

ODE TO THE BIALEK CLUB

Our Club, named for Chaim Nachman Bialek,
Baltimore boys who were never bucolic.
      A great statesman and poet,
         Our meetings would show it.
At our shore parties there was great frolic.

Our president, Henry Cohen,
Than whom there is none better known,
      He brings us together
         In all kinds of weather,
Be it sunny, or rainin', or snowin'.

Our advisor, Lou Schwartzman, would guide us.
It's a wonder he could abide us.
      But he showed his deep caring
         And wisdom by sharing
Rich values with which he plied us.

Leon Lerner's our resident poet,
Philosopher, too, and you know it.
      Shy he is not.
         He'll debate on the spot.
Published a book -- he'll gladly show it.

Then there's Woolf, whom we call Len,
Whose voice outshines his pen.
      He can daven - zayer zees
         We listen without surcease,
To hear him again and again.

Herb Silver and Belle, his bride,
Are celebrating 50 with pride.
      We wish them well,
         Far more than we can tell.
With true love, walking side by side.

Our "Thank you" to Jerry Schuman,
A real mensh, a genuine human.
      Shake his hand, what the heck
         As he picks up the check.
We hope that his assets keep bloomin'.

Then there's one whom we call Izz,
At acting, something of a whiz.
    Though he went into teaching
      He always was reaching
For Broadway, the heart of show biz.

If I continue thus one by one,
You know that we'll never get done.
    So hail to the rest,
      They're surely the best.
Jewish boys who will not be outdone.

Henry Hyman and Ethel, his wife,
Harry Korsover -- have a good life.
    Jerry Cooper, be well,
      Ben Erlich, you're swell.
Bob Gerber - we'll all weather the strife.

Charles Epstein - he's on the list.
And Bob Rosensteen, he can't be missed.
    Hessie Glasser, too,
      And you, and you.
All great club maven, I insist.

If there's any here I've omitted,
It's an error innocently committed.
    I apologize deeply,
      It was unintended completely.
When we meet next, your crown will be fitted.

I bring you one piece of good news.
The Bialek Club will not raise its dues.
    No big deal for astronomy,
      But a boost for Clinton's economy.
We're all winners - no one will lose.

We Bialek boys, growing up Jewish,
Lovely wives who are never shrewish.
    After 60 years - we still meet,
      A spirit you can't beat.
L'Chaim -- that's my true wish.

June 15, 1994

A TRIBUTE TO JULES AT EIGHTY

I have a brother named Jules.
In psychology he knows all the rules.
      When they don't exist
      He will vigorously persist
To create his own new tools.

A guy named Jim came to see.
The Case of Jim came to be.
      Jules has got what it takes,
      The pamphlet sold like hot cakes;
Now the rest is history.

While teaching, he set up his shop.
New products came in non-stop.
      Like bees to honey,
      Orders flew in, with money.
Jules' reputation rose to the top.

Then business grew rougher and rougher,
Other projects began to suffer.
      So he sold, in due course,
      With royalties, of course,
Providing a financial buffer.

On Wall Street, his stocks rose in spurts.
With futures he even flirts.
      Then along came Portside
      And the end of his pride,
As all of us lost our shirts.

Still there's one thing Jules didn't buy.
Derivatives - don't give them a try.
      Orange County went broke,
      And that's surely no joke.
Don't just kiss your good money goodbye.

All the while, Jules kept up his writing,
Publishing papers - that was exciting.
      All about non-directive,
      Carl Rogers - quite effective.

Personality search was delighting.

Though Will was the first with a book,
Jules was not to be overtook.
    He assembled his writings,
      With their footnotes and citings.
Personality Integration was the form that it took.

There was Jules, and brothers three,
And of course, the lonely Gussie.
    We felt close, that was sure,
      Growing up in Baltimore.
Just one big happy family.

Family always meant much to you.
Love for Mom and Pop grew and grew.
    You admired Gussie and Will
      And I'm sure you do still,
As their memories keep them in view.

Of course, there's the ultimate test
Of your place in the family nest.
    Like the brothers Smothers
      And like lots of others,
I claim Mom always loved you the best.

Without Esther, your tale's not complete,
And Larry and Brad at your feet.
    Though life has its glitches,
      They're your life's true riches,
It's they who make your life sweet.

Which brings us to this day, old boy.
Our gathering is not just a ploy.
    Now that you're eighty
      We wish you days less weighty.
Good health, and very much joy.

          April 17, 1995

ODE TO SHIRLEY AT 75

There once was a young girl named Shirley,
Who wished that her hair were more curly.
      She shampooed and teased,
        But she never was pleased.
Now you know why she gets up so early.

Her preferred name's her middle name, Dena.
That would put her in a whole new arena.
      But with Izz and Sam,
        We don't need another scam.
Both with two names would be a misdemeanor.

One morning in 1918
She decided to enter this scene.
      The second of four,
        She soon ended the war.
There was less than one month in between.

Baltimore was the place she was born.
September 23 was the morn.
      To Ralph and to Rose,
        Who we surely suppose
Felt such joy that they tooted their horn.

She excelled in her lessons at school
Finished three years in two, and that's cool!
      But the family was poor
        Which determined for sure
After high school, work was the rule.

Yet she yearned for more education,
So to Hopkins at night with elation
      She enrolled in world history,
        A course, by some mystery,
I, too, chose to take - strange concatenation!

You may question the power of fate,
But there's one way to catch a mate.
      Take a course at college
        And you gain more than knowledge.
In fact, it's the perfect bait.

So in '42 Shirley was wed.
No B.S., an MRS. instead.
    Now you know the start
    Of how I lost my heart.
As Shirley to the altar was led.

But that did not end her yearning
To pursue her love for learning.
    She took nursery school training
    And succeeded in gaining
Credentials in the direction she was turning.

To school in New York we went,
One year in Ann Arbor we spent.
    She helped pay my way
    Teaching at Perry School each day
To pay back the money we were lent.

In '49 Washington beckoned.
It was worth a gamble, we reckoned.
    In Silver Spring's shade,
    With the friends that we made,
We've not regretted it, not for one second.

Then came David and Jonny and Phil,
With one grandchild, and more to come still.
    Our family has grown
    With the love we have known.
How better our lives to fulfill.

But there's still more that needs reciting.
Mental health Shirley found most exciting.
    Only eight they could take,
    She was one, no mistake.
The program proved most delighting.

Shirley worked at Area C.
And still works at RSVP.
    What a remarkable life,
    A great mother, and wife,
No one knows it better than me.

Now she's reached milepost 75.

But it's not just staying alive.
        The love of family and friends,
        The message that sends
Is the joy for which we all strive.

                September 1993

ON OUR 50TH

There once was Shirley and Izz.
At marriage they were quite a whiz.
      Love endured 50 years,
        Through joy and through tears.
He knew he was hers, she was his.

Both said, "I know who I am."
Sometimes a lion, then a lamb.
      But they did play the game
        Called "What's my name?"
When was he Izz, and when Sam?

Shirley taught nursery school,
Playtime, yes, but with the golden rule.
      Children were her first love,
        Pleasure and pay hand in glove,
You know that Shirley's no fool.

Then she studied in mental health,
Quite openly, using no stealth.
      Counseling parents of the young,
        Quite troubled, unstrung.
Rewarding, but no chance for wealth.

Then she switched to RSVP.
What that means is you and me.
      Elders all, volunteers,
        Helping others, three cheers
For the service they render, all free.

She helped Izz get his master's degree,
Public health it was destined to be.
      Then they left Baltimore
        For a job paying more.
That's what brought them here to D.C.

Health and welfare's the name of the game.
Serving people with pride, not with shame.
      Planned community service
        With conviction, not nervous.
Meeting needs of the poor and the lame.

We were more than husband and wife
    With all of its pleasures and strife.
    Dave and Jonny were born,
    And then Philip one morn,
The three sons to whom we gave life.

At first there were diapers to change,
Then bar mitzvah and college to arrange.
    We'll go broke, what the hell,
    Let's send Dave to Cornell,
A world quite different and strange.

For Jonny American U, close to home,
Off to Oberlin Philip did roam.
    We got one Ph.D.
    And a public administrator to be
And a computer whiz, bright as chrome.

Dave went to Boston, no fool he
With the sheepskin that read Ph.D.
    Counseling was his profession
    Moving up in progression
In his field of psychology.

At B.U. he met someone just great.
There's no doubt it was planned by fate.
    Counseling, too, was her field,
    Kathy by name, Ph.D. on her shield.
You guessed it, she became his mate.

Philip went off to L.A.
A fine place to work and to play.
    When he met Diane
    He concocted his plan.
Together they soon set the day.

Jonny waited, somehow he knew
That right women are rare and few.
    But then one for him came,
    It was Kathy by name,
Now we have Kathy one, Kathy two.

Now we live under a wonderful aura,
We have a first grandchild, *ken ahara*.
    We shout out with pride
    Of the joy we can't hide,
For the beautiful, lovable Laura.

At this point our story ends.
Who knows what the future portends?
    One thing sure is true,
      Shirley and I are grateful to you.
Thanks and love to our family and friends.

ODE TO SHEP

There was a great guy we call Shep,
Who walked with both vigor and pep.
    He's a wiz at toastmasters,
      He teaches like a pastor.
He progresses at work , step by step.

Let's celebrate, now he is fifty.
He's rich in great values, yet thrifty.
      He's respected at FEMA.
      He's practical, yet a dreamer.
He's a guy everyone calls nifty.

So let's all say hail to Shep
.Of the Willners he's a great rep.
      Is he friendly and hearty?
      Is he the life of the party?
If you ask me, I'd say "Yep"!

ON HER DEATH

LOOKING BACK

Now I cannot tell her how deeply I loved her – and love her still.
Her body lies beneath this small plot of earth where I stand.
She cannot see my tears, hear my weeping, feel my grief.

Did I tell her, when I could, of my love?
Why did I not, when I should, grasp her close to my breast?
Did I ask her to forgive my anger and my harsh words?
Did I say I am sorry when I should?

I look back with painful regrets,
But I cannot go back.
Go back and say what should have been said,
Do what should have been done.

Hurt as it will, the past is passed, and cannot be relived.
She cannot know how deeply I regret.
I whispered of my love that should have been shouted.

Now I stand here and tell the heavens and the earth
What I cannot tell her.

NEVER

Never is such a long time.
Never to see her again.
Never is so deep.
Never is so final.
Never again to walk with her, to talk with her.
Never is such pain.
Never to hold her, never to kiss her.
Never.

February 12, 2006

EMPTY

The apartment, our house, is empty – without her.
So empty.
The house is full of memories of her – everywhere.
Yet it is empty, barren, deserted.
Her clothes hang in the closet; her sweaters fill the chest – but she is not here to wear them.
It is so empty.
Her jewelry sits in their boxes, so neglected.
Her favorite necklace in those last days torments me.
She is not here who should be here with me, leaving me empty.
Her toothbrush stares at me, unused.
I roam from room to room where she walked, and spoke, she read, she slept beside me in our bed, where I am now alone.
I am so alone in our empty home.

February 12, 2006

STILL ME

I must remember – I am still me.
Through all those years, she was close to me,
      she was part of me, as I was such a part of her.
Now she has been torn from me.
She is not here with me, as she always was.
Now I am alone.
Desolate. Unconsoled. Lonely. And in grief.
Yet I am still me.

Deep down I know – life is to be lived.
Life must have its own aim; life must have a purpose.
Deep down I know this, beneath my pain and anguish and solitude.
I must bring it to the fore.
I must know – that I am still me.
I am without her.
My life has changed, yet I am still me.

February 12, 2006

DEATH

Death is a thief.
It stole the one I loved away from me,
Leaving me the poorer and alone.

Death is heartless.
It cares not how much pain and sorrow it brings to me,
How much my heart breaks.

Death is cruel.
It inflicts suffering and agony,
And is oblivious to its consequence.

Death is a destroyer.
It broke the partnership and leaves me alone,
In solitude, abandoned and deserted.

Death is a monster.
It attacks with no compassion,
Causing grief and sadness.

Death is forever.
It bars any hope, any return, any future,
It extends beyond comprehension.

Death is the master.
It will have its way,
And yield to no price or no appeal.

Death has its sting.
It is the one inevitable in our lives.

May 1, 2006

I AM ONE

I am one.

I lived as one-half of two
And now I am one.

I have discovered a new mathematical principle:
One is much much less than one-half of two.

One is incomplete,
Less than whole.

One is barren.

One wanders without aim or purpose,
Lost and alone.

I arrive for dinner and the host asks, "How many?"
"One", I reply.
Around me are many twos, mostly twos.
I was one of two;
Now I am one.

I am apart, different, separate,
Because I am one.

Nature needs two;
Only two can give life and create future generations.

One feels little joy;
Beauty needs to be shared;
Words need to be exchanged;
Appreciation must be spoken.

One is sad.

May 13, 2006

MOTHER'S DAY

I cannot tell her how much I love her,
This Mother's Day,
For she lies in the earth,
Unable to hear my words,
Or see my tears.

She was a mother to our three sons,
Who, with me, mourn her all days,
And today more, on Mother's Day.

For they acknowledge that she was a loving mother,
Who cared so much, and gave so much,
And set her standards so high,
She said she could not reach them.

She chided herself for coming short,
Yet she was so warm, so caring, so loving.
She had joy when they were happy,
And pain when they strayed.

And now it seems ended, since she died,
And was buried in the unfeeling earth.
Yet her love lives on, as does mine.
Our sons, and their son and daughters remember her
With love.
With precious memories of good days,
And deep love.

This is their first Mother's day without their mother,
And mine without my wife,
Who was the mother of our sons.
We mourn, deeply,
And search for the solace that remembered love might bring.

May 14, 2006

WITHOUT HER

Beauty must be shared.
With her there is such beauty,
Beauty in a multicolored sunset over the ocean,
Beauty in a flower,
Beauty in two birds watching their nest.
Without her there is no beauty in beauty.

Music must be shared.
With her Beethoven's sound is heavenly.
Mozart sings.
The orchestra carries you away.
Without her there is no music in music.

Words must be shared.
With her there is such common language.
There can be communication without words.
Thoughts reach out and touch each other.
Without her there are no words.

A poem must be shared.
With her a poem can tell of depth and promise.
A poem can express great joy,
Or plumb the pain of sadness.
Without her there is no poetry.

Life must be shared.
With her life is full of meaning.
Without her what is the meaning of life?

May 17, 2006

THE UNSEEN COURTYARD

There is a beautiful new courtyard just outside my window.
I see it every morning when I awake.
It abuts an older courtyard and the two blend into one grand view.

There is a waterfall in the upper courtyard,
Leading to a trail of stillness that draws your eye to the new waterfall in the new courtyard,
The falls flowing into a small pond.
The neighbor ducks fly over the new buildings to enjoy the new pond.

I watched as each tree was planted, and there are many trees,
Varying in color and shape and height.
Each tree was carefully planted, and fit into a well-thought-out design.

There is a special grove of four trees at the base of the pond.
I call this Shirley's Grove.

To give added grace to the scene, the architect designed plots of soil, plots of different shape and size, plots planted with a wide variety of low plants.

Around the courtyard there is a winding path,
That passes by the waterfalls and pond.

There are well-placed benches throughout the path, and two facing each other at the pond.

I watched as each smalll section of grass sod was placed next to each other section of grass sod, until the barren earth was all covered in green.

Each morning the automatic spinklers open and irrigate the grass and the trees and the plants,
To keep them alive and fresh and green.

All of this beauty was promised to Shirley when we moved to this abode.
We were told that from our window we would see a beautiful courtyard.

All that Shirley ever saw was rubble.
They were building the buildings, and needed a place to discard the scrap.
A fence encircled the barren ground to keep us out of the ugly work area.
The ugly work area was all she ever saw.

I look out in the beautiful courtyard Shirley has never seen, and never will see.
It brings me pain each morning.
I see the beauty she never saw, and it is unbeautiful in my eye.

It is sad, and it hurts so.

Shirley's Grove is there, but it is unseen.
The beautiful courtyard is there, but it is unseen.
I know that what I see is unseen.

May 20, 2006

WHY?

Birth, life, love, offspring, and death,
This is the cycle ordained for us, one and all.
There is no escape.
Joy there may be, and pain for us all.

We come in with only what we inherit, each his own.
Before we leave, we ask, each one – what have I left for those still to come?

What law or power sets this course, we cannot know,
Only that it is so.
What power each possesses we seek to exercise,
Yet we are bound by the limits of our inheritance and our growing.

I set this down, as I must, to assuage my grief,
Grief for her who now lies in the earth, away from me.
Her I loved so, and with whom I lived so long, and conceived our sons.
Alone now to live out my allotted time, alone.
I set this down to calm my pain.
I set this down to understand what none can understand.
Why must she die and leave me?
Now I know – it is thus ordained.

July 1, 2006

ME

I am me.
I must be me.
Alone now, yes, for she has gone, not to return.
I am sad, and I grieve.
Yet I know and I must know that I am here, and I am me.
I am what remains of we two; thus it is.
So I must be me, remaining me.

Without her, I am less, yet I am me.
I must be me.
Try, I must, to stand straight and tall, though diminished without her.
Try, I must, to go forward, remembering what's past and cannot return.
Forward with my ambitions, my aims, my goals.
These I still possess, though I have lost her to share them.
Forward I must go,
For I must know and believe that I am me.
He, still, who shared all with her, yet remained the inherent me.
So I am me.

July 4, 2006

NOT 90

I don't want to believe I'm 90 years old.
Have I really lived that long?
I don't remember it all.
Not really.
Surely I can't have lived 90 years.
Not that long.

I don't want to believe I'm 90.
There's too much still to do.
That's too much past,
Not enough ahead.
I need more time.

I can't believe it.

I don't want to believe I'm a widower.
Did she really die?
I don't want to be living alone.
I still need my wife.
My life without her – it is too lonely, too empty, too sad.

I don't want to believe – but it seems I must.
I am 90, and I have the papers to prove it.
I am living alone, and I have the tears to prove it.

There is a road ahead, I can see.
Fortunate I am with family to travel it with me.
My three sons, beautiful of mind and beautiful of spirit,
And rich with my love.
Their lovely wives;
And my beautiful grandchildren – through whom my memory will live on.

Thus, at some small measure of peace, I celebrate 90.

July 5, 2006

SHE DIED

Lonely, quiet, sad.
People ask, and I say, "She died."
I now know grief.
It cuts deep inside.

How I yearn for the times with her.
Couples walk by, and I am alone.
I watch the couples, and I remember holding her hand.
We sat together on a bench in the park, we two.
I sit alone.
Emptiness.
Hollow.
Barren.
Deep solitude.

It is quiet; no voice calls my name, as she did.
It is lonely.
She died.
I am sad.

July 8, 2006

BY SHIRLEY'S GROVE

I sit alone by Shirley's grove.
In the courtyard outside my window, a cluster of trees,
Beside a small pool and waterfall.
Quiet, serene.
It is half a year since she was lowered into her grave,
And I sit alone.

I recall –
How I held her, kissed her, sat with her, talked with her, ate with her, slept with her, and cried with her.
Now no more.
I sit alone by Shirley's grove,
Half a year since she left me.
And I sit alone.

July 23, 2006

FLOWERS ON HER GRAVE

I placed flowers on her grave today.
I know she does not know.
But I know.

Half a year ago we lowered her into her grave;
We covered her coffin with the earth,
The earth I now touch, to be as near to her as I can be.

My thoughts are wholly with her,
My voice speaks to her because I know.
I know I must tell her how I love her still,
She must know how I miss her each day.

I was drawn to her grave today.
I placed flowers on her grave,
And spoke to her, in my way.
I know.

THE DEATH ALPHABET

Death decrees absence, aloneness, abiding and deep.
Death asks: what is beyond the grave?
Death is a cruel cessation of the wonders of life; it teaches men to cry.
Death creates a desolate spirit.
Death leaves empty spaces everywhere.
Death breaks up a family.
Death tells you the one you loved is gone; it reveals God's plan for the price of birth and life.
Death opens hollow holes.
Death demands a new independence.
Death is a journey whose course we do not fathom.
Death knows no end.
Death sounds a lonely lament.
Death pleads for a lasting memorial.
Death declares that you will never again be with the one you loved.
Death opens unhealed wounds.
Death brings sharp pains.
Death leads to quiet hours alone.
Death leaves the senses raw.
Death produces a pervasive silence, the silence of empty rooms.
Death opens a flood of tears.
Death is the ultimate unknowable.
Death cuts a deep void.
Death opens a gaping wound.
Death is the master x, the great unknown.
Death recalls all of the yesterdays.
Death is the zenith of life's last breath.

September 2006

NOT GOOD-BYE

She, whom I loved,
Loved so deeply, and loved so enduring,
She lives no more.
She, who was Shirley
Is no more.

She was my life.
She was my wife.
Alone, now, all alone,
I am bereft.

I never said good-bye.
I will not and cannot say good-bye,
For she is with me every day, in many ways.
That empty space beside me in my bed,
At breakfast alone, she stares at me from her smiling photo.
At lunch in the café where we often met, I stare at the empty chair.
At the concert where we shared such joy, there is an empty seat next to me.
As I drive alone, I touch the soft felt in the seat beside me,
I reach over and touch
As I often reached over and touched her.

She is with me and of me and in me still.

October 2006

I AM CONSOLED

Shirley died.
My life was with Shirley, and for Shirley.
We shared each other more than six decades.
I loved Shirley so much; no man can love a woman more deeply.
Shirley died, and I miss her – every day.

How do I go on living, this new life alone, all alone?
How do I live without Shirley?

Amid all of the events of life in a day and a year, I am consoled.
I am consoled by one memory, one recollection, one phrase.

In her last illness, she awoke one night.
I was awake, caring for her, knowing she was near death.
Shirley said one thing only.
"I love you so much."
I am consoled.
I can go on living without her, as I must, with her memory.

November 1, 2006

IF SHE WERE HERE

If she were here,
If she were here with me
What I would do,
How I would feel,
How my world would be…..

If I could take her for a walk in the sunny courtyard,
I would take her hand and walk beside her in the sunny courtyard.

If she were here,
I would hold her close to me,
So close it would take her breath away,
If she were here.

If she were here,
That deep lonely feeling would not be,
The silence and the emptiness of the rooms would vanish,
To be filled with her.

At night I would have my companion beside me in my bed,
Not the solitude of now in a spacious bed hardly occupied.

If she were here,
I would love her so, and tell her I love her so.

If she were here…..

November 17, 2006

LOOKING FORWARD

Now I am alone.
I am I, I am me.
Alone, I must go forward.

I have changed , but the world has not.
The sun rises and the sun sets,
And the moon appears each night.
I gaze at it alone, yet it is the same moon.

There is work to be done,
And I must do my share.
There are wrongs to be righted,
And I am obliged to lend my weight.
There is music to hear, and beauty to take in.
There is a legacy to leave,
And I must account for it.
Each day is today.
Tomorrow can be reached only when it becomes today.
Day by day I am me.

She I loved has died, and I am changed and alone,
Yet, in my pain and grief, I must go forward.

SHIRLEY

Everything around me says "Shirley".
I stare at the picture, she and I.
She is in every room,
So she can be with me,
And I with her.
"Shirley" in the photograph.

That smile as she looks at her granddaughter,
It is so beautiful.
"Shirley" is so beautiful.
A beautiful and loving smile.
It brings tears to my eyes,
As I kiss "Shirley" in the picture.

Everything says "Shirley".
I hear the music, and the rhythm says "Shirley",
    Repeats, "Shirley" over and over, "Shirley", "Shirley",
      In time to the music.
The music was made for "Shirley".

"Shirley" will not leave my mind.
Everything says "Shirley".
I walk down the hall where we two walked,
Or I took her in her wheelchair
In the last months of her dying.

I walk in the courtyard, the courtyard she hoped to see,
And never saw.
I pause at the grove of trees, the grove I call "Shirley's" grove.'
It grows by the pond and the waterfall.
"Shirley:" would have loved the courtyard, the falls, the grove.
All say "Shirley".

I sit at the concert, and the chair next to me—
It is meant for "Shirley".
It says "Shirley".
Though it is empty.

Everthing says "Shirley".

CHAPTER II :

MARILYN

WITH YOU

Every moment is precious – with you.
Each moment becomes a precious hour – with you.
I love being with you.

Meals together – with you.
Walking – with you.
I love living day and night with you.

So much joy - - with you.
So much understanding -- we two.
Two who love.

I am with you.

August 11, 2007

PRECIOUS

Gold, they say, is precious, though I find nothing appealing about a 3- ounce bar of gold.

A diamond, I am told, is precious, and I know it is highly valued for some, but I find no attraction to a stone dug from the earth and called a diamond.

A genuine pearl grown in an oyster, I hear, is rare and precious and worth much, and I admit a pearl string around your neck adds much to the décor, but why it should be valued so highly is beyond me.

These, to many, are precious, but not to me.

To me, you are precious.
It is you I value.
Your face is precious.
Your lips are precious.
Your hair is precious.
Your hand in mine is precious.
Your mind is precious.
Your love is precious.
It is you who is precious to me.

February 15, 2009

WE HAVE EACH OTHER

How fortunate we are to have each other.

We are two together,
Who belong together.

Each, fulfilling the other.

We are a pair,
Who need to share,
And share we do.

Each gives to the other,
And each takes the best.

Together we fulfill.

Each alone is diminished;
Together we flourish.

We must believe it was meant to be.

How fortunate we are to have each other
In love.

October 24, 2007

HOW I MISS YOU

You are away,
And I miss you so much.

You are away,
And I am here without you
Alone, and lonely.

You are away,
And there is an emptiness.

Without you,
I am not wholly me.

There is so much missing –
It is you.

We are meant to be two,
Together.
One alone is incomplete.

I tell you,
How I miss you,
Deeply.

October 24, 2007

YOU ARE BEAUTIFUL

WHAT IS BEAUTY? WHAT IS BEAUTIFUL? FOR TWO?

BEAUTY IS LOVE.
BEAUTY IS TRUST.
BEAUTY IS OPENNESS.
BEAUTY IS CLOSENESS.
FOR TWO.

BEAUTIFUL IS A WALK ON THE BEACH.
BEAUTIFUL IS WATCHING THE MOON RISE.
BEAUTIFUL IS A MEAL TOGETHER.
BEAUTIFUL IS SHARING; SHARING ALL.
FOR TWO.

BEAUTY IS YOU AND I TOGETHER.
BEAUTY IS MY LOVE FOR YOU.

AUGUST 31, 2007

THERE IS THE OCEAN

There is the Ocean
And there is you.

Wave on wave, ceaseless,
And the constant you.

Wide, wide shoreline
Me beside you.

Stretching to distant shores,
And just we two.

The sun rises over water,
I see it with you.

We walk on the boardwalk,
We two.

There is the Ocean,
And me and you.

I love the Ocean,
And I love you.

June 26, 2007

VALENTINE'S DAY

It's Valentine's Day,
A special time to say I love you.

I think it every day,
Feel it in every way,
So it's a joy to tell you today.

If I were near to you now,
There'd be more than words. I vow
You would feel the depth of my love.

From this distance I must be content
To send the message I've sent.
Now you know what my heart conveys.

Be happy on Valentine's Day
And be my Valentine.

February 14, 2007

MISSING YOU

When do I miss you?

I miss you when I awake in the morning.
No, I miss you while I sleep.
I miss you at breakfast.
I miss you when I read the paper,
And want to tell you what I think of the terrible news.

I miss you for lunch.
I miss you all afternoon,
When we could take a pleasant walk – together.

I miss you when I listen to good music,
Which you could share.

I miss you at dinner,
For the two of us;
When I am bored by the empty women at the table.

I miss you watching the news after dinner.
To hear what you think of the news.

I miss you when I go to bed.
I miss you all day, every day.

Because I love you.

January 2007

WE TWO THIS SUMMER

We two this summer.

Together this summer, all summer.

Summer at the Oceanside.

On warm days and cool nights,

We two.

We two alone, or joining friends.

We two together.

We walked on sand by the ocean, and walked on water and waves.

We dipped in the pool.

We ate on the deck and dined in luxury.

We tracked the moon.

At 4:00 a.m. we tracked the shuttle in space.

We walked the boardwalk, hand in hand.

We two shared our love – all summer, this summer. We two.

BEFORE AND AFTER

Before. Before I met Marilyn, I was alone.
After. After I met Marilyn I felt a part of two.

Before, I had my thought, but no one to express them to.
After, I have someone to share my thoughts with.

Before, I worked to prove to myself I was still vital and productive.
After, I can share my work with someone who will appreciate my efforts.

Before, I saw a dark future, a life alone.
After, I have a vision of life together with someone I love, and who loves me.

January 2007

LONGING

There is a deep and pervasive feeling of longing,
    Longing to be with you.
Longing to hold you, touch you.

I long to hear your voice,
    A sweet sound, comforting, warm and pleasing.

I long to kiss you,
    So you will know I love you.

The distance stands between us.
    I yearn to close it, to reach out and I am with you.

The time stands between us.
    I yearn to close it, to have you, now.

I will bear the longing,
    Because I know I will be with you, and tell you again – I love you.

January 2007

TO MARILYN

When she and he together share this life,
Knowing they must endure what fate decrees,
Prepared to endure pain, tragedy, and strife,
To weather cold and dark stormy seas.

Yet filled with hope instead, great joy to know
From stress and trial and pressure find surcease,
To plant the seeds of happiness, to grow,
From all that may be befall to find calm peace.

Then know the immutable law decreed above,
Life is a journey meant for two,
At heart all that befalls depends on love,
And love knows but one master – you.

If you'd be loved, that love yourself must earn,
Only the love you give comes back in rich return.

February 26, 2007

WE TWO

Two paths are open to each of us.
We can choose, as most do, to find a mate – one who enriches our lives, with whom we spend our years together, with its joys and its trials, yet in all, a wondrous journey.
Or we can live alone, in all, a lonely journey.

All too often, on this path, as years go by, that awesome phrase each has spoken to the other in our union – "'till death do us part" – becomes real, and once again, one is alone. Most often it is she, alone. Visit any of the many communities of retirement, and observe those alone – she most often.

Two paths are again open to each of us, though less open than the paths of youth.
How fortunate, then, are we, to have found each other. Those lonely years, those times of solitude, are behind us. We are now two who have found each other.

Learning, again, how two live together. Is she without flaws? Am I? All that we have learned and lived over the long years is still with each of us. So we learn, again, of life for two – sharing, caring, forgiving, and yes –new love.

November 27. 2007

I AM LOVED

You must hear my message.
You must listen to my words,
You must feel the passion.

Reciprocal is my theme.

How I love you.
I love you deeply, fully, unconditionally.
And what joy it is to love.
It fulfills.
Loving is so enriching.
Loving is life.

Turn the coin over, and discover the reciprocal –
I am loved.
What utter joy – to be loved.
To be loved – no greater passion can be felt.
How enriching it is to be loved.
How fulfilling.
To be loved is life.

July 22, 2007

I AM NOT ALONE

I am not alone.
Marilyn is there for me, loving me, always.
There are times of joy together.
But there are times, too, of anxiety and troubled thoughts.
It's then I know – I am not alone. Marilyn is there for me, loving me.

When I cannot sleep, and lie restless and troubled,
It's then I know – I am not alone.
Marilyn is there beside me, for me, loving me.

I am not alone, because I have someone I love – Marilyn

And I am not alone.

January 17, 2011

MARILYN AND THE SKY

You'll find Marilyn looking up, up at the moon.
Just about every night.
When it's full, each month, it's more exciting.
She looks longer, more deeply, at the full moon.
Marilyn depends on the moon.
Each night, each month.
And a full moon caps it off.

You'll find Marilyn looking across, across the lake, at the sunset.
Each night the lake and the sunset call to her, and she responds.
Tonight it is pink and blue and grey as the clouds catch the fading rays.
A beautiful sunset sinks into her mind.
Marilyn loves the sunset, across the lake.
The lake reflects the sunset.

You'll find Marilyn looking up, up at the clouds.
Florida clouds are different than New Jersey clouds and Maryland clouds.
Each has its unique qualities, fully described by Marilyn.
Marilyn appreciates the clouds of the sky.

You'll find Marilyn in synch with the natural world and its wonders, its beautiful wonders.
The sunset, the moon, and the clouds.
These are Marilyn's beauties.